For Nancy

Contents

Your
Name
in Print

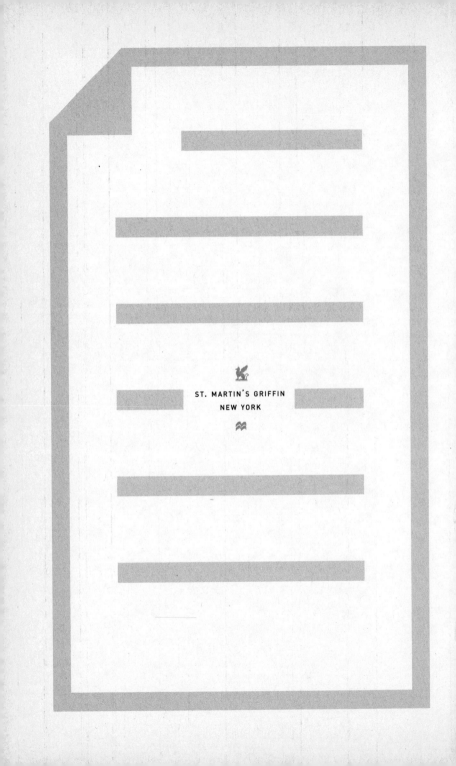

ST. MARTIN'S GRIFFIN
NEW YORK

Acknowledgments

We have a lot of people to thank, starting with Marian Lizzi, the editor who came up with the idea for the book and encouraged us to pitch it to St. Martin's Press. We also owe a debt of gratitude to Julie Mente, the St. Martin's editor who guided our book through the writing and production process.

Many professional writers helped us, sharing tips and advice, especially Kelly James-Enger and Sally Wendkos Olds, along with Jim Morrison, Amy Zipkin, and other members of the American Association of Journalists and Authors who provided assistance. We're also grateful to the teen writers who shared their experiences and insights with us.

At home, Lizzie's mom, Nancy Bobrowitz, feathered the nest—Tim's office, at the top of our house—and offered welcome moral support. She also provided invaluable suggestions in editing our drafts. And the lunches she prepared for the three of us to eat out on the porch were always a highlight of the work day. Lizzie's brother Jonny, Tim's unofficial computer support department, chipped in and helped whenever we had a technical problem. He also took over Lizzie's usual lawnmowing duties during the summer that she was working on the book.

Finally, people warned us that we'd be at each other's throats, that working together would sorely test the good father-daughter relationship we've always had. Consequently, we were prepared for some tension, but we're happy to report there was very little. The whole process went as smoothly as we had hoped, and we got along great throughout. So most of all, we'd like to thank each other for making this such an enjoyable project.

Elizabeth Harper
Timothy Harper
Ridgewood, New Jersey

Introduction

THE IDEA behind this book is that it's never been easier for young writers to get their work published—or more important for them. Our book advises teenagers, their parents, and their teachers how to go about writing something that is worthy of being published, and then guides them through the steps to actually get their work into print. We cast a wide net: from school newspapers to *The New York Times* to books; from the local weekly to *USA Today*; from a blog on a homemade Web site to Salon.com; from comics to poetry to journalism to essays to sci-fi novels. Our goal is to encourage, to inspire, to show that it is possible for anyone who writes well to get published and be read. And, most important, to lay out the specifics of how it can be done.

We're a father-daughter team. Timothy, whom everybody calls Tim, is a longtime journalist, author, foreign correspondent, and educator. This is his twelfth book. His eighteen-year-old daughter Elizabeth, whom everybody calls Lizzie, was an editor of her high school newspaper, and was a columnist for the weekly newspaper in Ridgewood, New Jersey. During high school she also occasionally contributed to the Bergen County (N.J.) *Record*, the metropolitan daily paper that serves the northern New Jersey suburbs of New York, and she was published in *The New York Times*. In writing this book in the months before Lizzie left home for her freshman year at Oberlin College in Ohio, we tried to offer a mix of straightforward explanation of how the writing world works, along with advice on how young readers/writers can make it work to their advantage. And the advantages of getting published are what the book is all about: better grades, self-esteem, status, influence in the community, maybe some spending money, and a credit that truly stands out on a college application.

In addition to practical how-to writing advice, we've collected insights from experts, writers, editors, publishers, parents, teachers, and others; "at a glance" mini-profiles of young writers; and little individual riffs—"Tim Says . . ." and "Lizzie Says . . ."—when and where it is appropriate for one of us to be offering our individual point of view rather than speaking with a combined voice. We thought it would be important not only to tell you what we've done and how we've done it, but to tell you what others have done, too. We also thought it would be important to include real-life samples; you'll know what a publishable op-ed piece, a well-received local weekly column, a successful magazine query, and a satirical piece printed in the *New York Times* look like because we'll show them to you.

By all evidence, the number of kids who are writing–writing something, anything, everything–is growing. Whether in the school newspaper or a blog (Web log) or music lyrics or a secret journal hidden under the mattress, this is a generation that has grown up not learning by rote memorization, but by being told stories. In school, virtually all learning exercises–history, languages, culture, even math–are now taught in story form. The popularity of reality TV is no mystery: people want to see real stories about real people, and how they come out.

Kids today recognize the power of the story, and many of them are experimenting with storytelling on their own. They recognize that storytellers are stars, and writing can lead to fame and fortune. Few of them can be Tim Burton, but nearly all of them can scribble in a notebook or tap on a computer keyboard. We'll concede that not all those kids who are experimenting with writing want to publish their work. But how many people really write only for themselves? We're convinced, and thankful, that the vast majority of kids think they have something to say, think other people will be interested in what they have to say, and like the idea of having other people admire and appreciate their writing. It is easier than ever to get published, but make no mistake—it is still difficult. There are more potential places than ever for teens to publish, but finding the right publication can still be daunting.

In some ways, however, the message of this book is that getting published is less important than the process, discipline, and goals involved in writing. Even for teenagers who don't want to be professional writers—even for teens who really don't care whether they ever get published anywhere beyond their school paper—writing is something that can stretch their creativity and help them find their niche, and it's fun. More than anything, we hope our book helps teenagers learn to be creative and expressive, and to appreciate good writing, whether it's their own or someone else's.

This book is not only for the kids who have already marked themselves out as the best writers in their schools, the kids who are already the stars of the school paper. We are aiming at every kid who writes or wants to write—and we recognize that not all those kids are on the staff of their school papers. Think about it. Often, the most creative kids, the ones who write exhaustive blogs on LiveJournal.com or scrawl comic books or dream up elaborate science fiction worlds are not the ones who fit easily onto the staff of a school newspaper. But they are just as interested—and often more likely to find success—in getting published. This book is for any young writer who dreams of seeing his or her byline in print, and having other people read his or her words.

For many writers and would-be writers, getting published has an almost mystical appeal. There's something about seeing your words in print, and knowing that they can inform and influence people, or sometimes even make people laugh. When your writing has been published and can be read by virtually anyone in the world who picks up the newspaper or magazine or book or clicks on the web site, you're having an influence on the world. You're making a mark. We hope this book helps you make your mark.

A Note to Parents (and Teachers)

Parents can be extremely helpful to teenagers who want to break into print by suggesting story ideas and reading over or editing young writers' work. Parents who know people in the media can introduce their kids to them, or take their aspiring writers to newsstands and help them pick out magazines that they need to read before deciding where to submit their stories. Parents can provide the computers and the Internet connections that link young writers to the world, and parents take kids on vacations that help young writers see the world and write travel stories about it for newspapers back home.

Let's make one point clear: Writing is not for everybody. It's not easy. It's hard, sometimes very hard, and occasionally impossible. Under any circumstances, it can be a lot of work. Not every kid is a writer, or wants to be a writer, or can be a writer. Parents should never push or force too hard for their children to write, and especially to write something specifically for publication. However, parents who think their kids might be good writers or might get published some-day should encourage them and help them find the opportunities to write.

Offer constructive, positive criticism—as long as it remains constructive and positive. But even if a parent is helping the young writer improve, the parent should back off if the kid doesn't appreciate the help. Don't worry, Mom or Dad. Your young writer can and will find the kind of feedback he or she needs somewhere, from someone else. Parents shouldn't expect their twelve-year-olds or even their eighteen-year-olds to produce writing like the stories in *The New Yorker* or *Time* magazine. Even if their kids' writing is flawed—and whose isn't, in some way, especially when just starting to write?—parents should stay positive and find ways to compliment their kids and keep them writing. After all, the writing is the main thing, not the getting published. Getting into print is a bonus.

Your
Name
in Print

GETTING PUBLISHED:
What Clips and Credits
Can Do for You

W HY SHOULD YOU TRY to get published? What will you gain?

First, of course, is the fact that writing more—and trying to write well enough to get into print—will lead to writing better, and working smarter and more efficiently. That usually leads to better grades in school, which both parents and kids like, and it can lead to more time for extra work and, even better, more time for friends, hobbies, and leisure. Yes, good writing takes time, more than poor writing. But good writing actually creates more time for ourselves in the long run; if you do a good job on a piece of writing, for example, that usually means you don't have to spend as much, if any, time rewriting later.

Beyond the immediate prospect of writing better papers and reports in high school, there's also the issue of college to consider—and not just the application essays. (Most students do one "master" essay for their college applications, but some schools require more than one, and many schools want an essay unique to their own application.) Beyond the essay, there's also the simple fact that colleges and universities today are looking for good communicators because they make better student leaders. If you've been published, you've proven yourself a good communicator, and that's a skill that will serve you well in college and for future success in virtually any career. Some careers are all about good writing; journalism is a good example. But in any career—public relations, business management, financial services, health care, education—being a good communicator, especially a good writer, is never going to be a drawback. Whether doing massive reports or interoffice e-mail memos, people who write effectively are the ones who gain the respect of supervisors, clients, and colleagues. Putting your ideas and points together in a cohesive, compelling manner, are critical to success. If you can write well, you will have an advantage.

Being a published writer also gives you a leg up over other applicants trying for the same spots in the freshman class, especially at the most selective colleges. Admissions counselors at top schools across the country consistently say they look for something that makes a student stand out, something different and unusual. At some top schools it can seem like every applicant is captain of a varsity team or editor of the yearbook or a

4.0 student, and everybody has done lots of amazing community service. But very few will have had a column in the local weekly newspaper, or articles published in the larger regional newspaper, or even *The New York Times*. Lizzie has, and there is no doubt that those publication credits—along with her essay—and school performance helped when she applied for early admission to Oberlin College in Ohio, which is one of the the top liberal arts schools in the country. (She got in, by the way, which is a good thing since she didn't have even one backup school—and that's not something we would recommend.)

One admissions counselor we interviewed (he asked that we not give the name of his school, a selective liberal-arts college in the Midwest) told us that being published, especially having written a book, "would say that the student can write and has gone out of their way to get a publishing contract and has a little bit of professional experience. Also, depending on who they're published by, it tells us that their writing has gone through an external review." The fact that an independent publisher (or even a newspaper, magazine, or Web site) would choose to print your writing—and maybe even pay you for it—is a stamp of approval.

Getting into print can raise your profile in the community, whether that community is made up of the students who read your school paper, fans who read music web sites, citizens who read the local daily newspaper, or cyber-surfers who keep up with your adventures and misadventures on your personal blog. When your works are published and people read them, you influence those readers. Your voice is heard. If you have something significant to say, if you make sense, people will pay attention. They'll talk about it. Sometimes it makes a difference.

For example, in the months after the attacks of September 11, 2001, the school district in Ridgewood, New Jersey, the town where we live in the New York City suburbs, canceled most student field trips indefinitely, especially those to Manhattan. It made sense at the time; twelve residents of our town died at the World Trade Center, and safety and security was foremost in everyone's mind. As the months went on, however, the ban on field trips made less and less sense. Students, parents, and teachers all wanted the trips to resume. After all, many residents of Ridgewood—including many of the students' parents—had resumed commuting into the city every day. Many students once again were going into the city with their parents or on their own, taking the bus or the train, and visiting the museums, theaters, art galleries, and concert halls that make New York City the cultural capital of our country. But the high school still refused the allow the schools to resume educational trips to the Bronx Zoo, plays on Broadway, or museums such as the Metropolitan Museum of Art.

Lizzie, then a junior at Ridgewood High School, started writing a column, "High School Beat," in our local weekly newspaper, the *Ridgewood News*, in the autumn of 2002. She wrote about all sorts of things happening at the school, and all sorts of issues that were on students' minds. By the spring of 2003, when the ban on field trips had been in effect for nearly a year and a half, she wrote a column saying it was time to let students take field trips again. The column appeared on a Friday, and many people in town were talking about it over the weekend. A couple of weeks later, she offered an expanded version of the piece to the opinion pages of the Bergen County *Record*, the large and influential daily newspaper that is distributed to much of northern New Jersey. The newspaper's opinion editor ran the piece, and it caused even more comment in Ridgewood, both in and out of the schools. We're sure her *Ridgewood News* column or her *Record* opinion piece, or both, were read by members of the school board and the school administrators—the people responsible for the policy. A short time later, the school district announced that it was rescinding the ban and that field trips to Manhattan would resume. Now, we can't say that Lizzie's articles were the main reason that field trips resumed. We can't say for certain that they had any impact at all. But we like to think they did. (What do you think? See her *Record* opinion piece on page 80.)

Beyond raising your profile in the community, getting published can be a great exercise in citizenship. There's a reason the Founding Fathers guaranteed freedom of speech and freedom of the press; they are critical to democracy. Making your voice heard, getting your opinions published, is a great way to participate in democracy. Any teenagers who complain that the "grown-up world" doesn't pay attention to them should pick up a pen or sit down at a keyboard and write a letter to the editor. If you want to be heard, speak up.

Speaking of citizenship and a higher profile in the community, those are characteristics that are particularly appealing to the people who select the winners of college scholarships and other awards. Your writing can pay off indirectly. Of course, it can also pay off directly if you get paid for your writing. We'll talk a lot more about where and how you can sell your writing, but for now, trust us: if you're a good writer and you have good ideas, it can happen. (Speaking of getting paid, we should note that while Lizzie got the personal satisfaction of seeing her articles published on the ban on field trips, the *Record* also paid her for it. In that instance, participating in democracy had a bonus: a couple of CDs and several items of clothing from the local vintage store.)

Along with the possibilities of income from part-time writing, who knows, maybe you'll find out that you love writing, or maybe even that you want to do it for a living someday. Tim can tell you that it is a rewarding life, traveling around the world meeting interesting people and seeing extraordinary events and then writing about them. Lizzie can tell you how selling a freelance piece here and there to earn money can be a lot more fun, and a lot easier, than the usual after-school or weekend job in a store or restaurant. Even if writing is strictly a hobby–keeping a journal, creating stories just for friends, or writing up family vacations for relatives–it can be extremely personally satisfying.

So grab whatever opportunity you have to write, and explore. Most writers start small, like with a school newspaper. Very few start off with the Great American Novel. Those small starts can often lead to great things. Just remember that getting published isn't the only goal or benefit for a young writer.

TIPS FROM AN ADMISSIONS EXPERT

Steven R. Antonoff heads his own Denver-based educational consulting firm. A big part of his job is looking at high school students' accomplishments, advising them on which colleges and universities might be best for them, and helping them put together an application that will increase their chances of getting admitted to the schools on the top of their list. He urges students to capitalize on their skills, especially if they are good writers.

Applications should provide the college admissions counselors with a sense of who the student is, and what he or she can accomplish, Antonoff says; being a published writer can be the sort of "hook" that helps an application stand out from the crowd. The higher the quality of clippings and published credits, the more weight they carry with admissions counselors. "There are plenty of students who are editors of student newspapers and who are decent writers," he says, "and, quite honestly, at most competitive colleges they're a dime a dozen. But if you have had something published in a significant magazine or newspaper or journal—whatever that means to a teenager—yes, you stand apart."

No matter where applicants have been published, however, Antonoff says that colleges look for students who have interesting experiences or perceptions of the world, and then can vividly describe them.

Lizzie Says:
WRITING OPENS DOORS

One benefit of writing a newspaper column was the recognition I got as a writer. I felt this most acutely in our own neighborhood, when adults I'd only met a few times before, maybe at the annual block party, would tell me they'd read my pieces in the paper. In more than one instance, my reputation as a writer led to an opportunity (and some money) I would not have gotten otherwise.

In the fall of my senior year, I was pleasantly surprised when a neighbor said she admired my writing and asked me to help her son with his application to a prestigious prep school. Being in the middle of the college application process myself, I agreed to help. When I went over to his house, Michael, an eighth grader, had already completed most of the application. He just needed to write a few sentences for each of the short answer questions, which asked things like, "What are your greatest strengths as a student?" and "Describe an interesting vacation you've taken." Michael knew the answers to these questions—he knew that he was persistent, that his favorite vacation was a trip to Ireland—but he needed to express them articulately and persuasively.

As an applicant, I know how hard it is to sit down and

praise yourself–talking, rather than writing, feels more natural. We talked for a while about why he felt he was a good match for this particular school, and he mentioned a number of valuable details that hadn't come up before. Our conversation got Michael's thoughts moving in the right direction so that he could translate his answers to me into carefully written responses. He did a good job on his application. He was pleased, as were his parents, and I was pleased when they paid me more than I expected.

About a month later, another neighbor asked me to help her daughter who was also applying to a private high school. The application was due in a few days, and everything but the essay was ready to go. Brenleigh just needed a little push. When I got there, I tried the same strategy I'd used with Michael: a casual conversation, aimed at getting her to open up and make observations she wouldn't have included otherwise. It worked again. After our chat, Brenleigh made some notes and added more personal information to her essay. The big message I tried to get through to her was that admissions officers don't really care about the specifics of your camping trip or vacation or whatever–they care about how the experience reflects on you. *You* are the focus of everything in your application.

I would have never expected that my own experiences as a writer and college applicant would lead to getting paid for helping other kids with their applications. Later on, I was even offered a regular job by an SAT tutor as a writing coach for her students. These were opportunities I'd never even considered, but because people had seen my writing in the paper, they trusted me to help their kids.

WHAT TO WRITE

So you want to be a writer. But what do you want to write? What kind of writing do you want to do? Where do you want to be published? Do you want to write stories for your school newspaper? For your town's local daily or weekly newspaper? For a regional magazine? For a national glossy like *Motor Trend* or *Jane*? Maybe you see yourself writing a novel, and someday doing a book signing at your local Barnes & Noble or appearing on *Oprah* to talk about your book. Or accepting the Oscar for Best Screenplay. Or giving a public reading from your first volume of published poetry.

Most of us, when we start out as writers, balance what we

want to write with what we *can* write and get published. Like so many other aspects of life and work and art, writing is often a balancing act: we want to aim high and achieve as much success as we can as quickly as we can, but we don't want to be unrealistic and overambitious. It's okay to hope to write a best-seller, but instead of sitting down and starting a big book maybe it's a good idea to start by writing some short stories. Baby steps are sometimes the way to go.

That's one of the best things about writing: there is no blueprint, no set path. But it's also one of the most maddening and frustrating things. Every writer has to find his or her own way, make his or her own mistakes, and stumble into his or her own successes. No one can tell you, hey, do it this way or do it that way. All anyone can do—as we're trying to do in this book—is present options and alternatives, and make suggestions. You try the ones that sound good, stick with the ones that feel comfortable and work for you, and discard the ones that don't. Another of the best—and worst—things about getting published is that the entry bar is so low. Education, experience, credentials, and connections typically do not matter as much in writing as in many fields, and sometimes credentials don't matter at all in getting published. Naturally, as in any other work, credentials and connections can help. For instance, you might be more likely to get a story published in the local paper if the editor is a neighbor and you have been babysitting for her kids for a long time.

Here's an example Tim uses in workshops and when coaching. He's been making a living as a writer for decades, and has written hundreds of articles for leading magazines and newspapers around the world. In the world of freelance writers, he's a seasoned pro. Lizzie, on the other hand, has had a few articles published, but is a relative novice. Suppose Lizzie and Tim each has an idea for a story for an airline magazine. Tim has had many stories published in the magazine and knows the editors well. Lizzie has never had a story published in any airline magazine, and the editors have no idea who she is. Tim sends in his story idea. Lizzie sends in hers. If Lizzie's idea is stronger than Tim's, the editors are going to tell Tim thanks but no thanks, try again. And they're going to send Lizzie a contract to do her story. In some businesses, people like to say you're only as good as what you did yesterday. In writing, you're only as good as what you're doing *now*.

Writing is also funny—funny weird, that is—in that anyone and everyone thinks he or she can do it. "Oh, you're a writer?" they say. "You know, I've been meaning to write a book, but I haven't had time." As if that's all it takes to become a writer. You never hear anyone tell a NASA physicist, "You know, I've been meaning to do some rocket science, too, but I haven't had the time." In truth, almost anyone can become a writer. But it takes more than time. And it takes more than good writing. You need to learn to come up with ideas for what to write about, to do the research, to organize the material, and, finally, to write it in a way that is informative, or entertaining, or both.

Can anybody do it? Sort of. Anybody can try to become a writer. Anybody can write something and show it to friends and relatives. Getting published is more complicated. And getting published in some places is more difficult than others.

That's why picking your spots is so important. What do you want to write? Where do you want to be published? Think long-term, of course. Aim high. Set some ambitious goals. Go ahead and envision your name on a poem in *The New Yorker,* or imagine yourself being interviewed on television about something you've written. Now, think about how you're going to get there. Or maybe you want to go ahead and aim high, but also set some closer, more easily accessible goals. Maybe your first goal is to get a byline in the school paper.

There's nothing wrong with either approach. For some people, it feels right to sit down right now and start writing that hoped-for bestseller. That's what some famous writers have done, including John Grisham with his first legal thriller and J. K. Rowling with her first Harry Potter book. Similarly, a number of teen authors, including some we mention in this book, started off by writing books that got published. But that's risky. Spending all your time and pinning all your hopes on a single opus is more likely to lead to disappointment. For every Grisham and Rowling—who were, we should point out, adults who had already mastered the basics of writing when they began working on their books—there are thousands of unknown, unpublished would-be authors whose manuscripts are buried forever in a drawer or a hard drive. Instead of aiming so high—bestseller or bust—maybe you want to try something else first. Maybe you're going to try a lot of something else first. That's the way most writers start, and the way that most of us progress. Sometimes it's two steps forward and one back. They key is to keep taking steps: the school paper, a blog, the local weekly, established Web zines, the big daily newspaper, poetry or literary journals, the regional magazine, the small niche publication, then bigger magazines, and ultimately books or screenplays. Whatever strategy or path you choose, be true to your own personality and style. Maybe you're not the sort of person who is interested in baby steps. Maybe you don't have the patience to wait years for success while writing a big novel—or to deal with the prospect of never getting published. Maybe you don't have the patience to deal with fellow students who turn into tyrants when editing your work for the school paper.

Whatever strategy you choose—and some people adopt more than one, and sometimes more than one at a time—don't forget what you're aiming for. A target is a powerful motivator. Set goals, short-term and long-term. Also, don't forget that becoming a writer, published or not, is more than a goal. It's a process, a journey. Writers learn something from everything they write, whether it's published or not, whether it's a big bestseller or a term paper that you got a C on. With every writing project, you will learn something about the subject, you will learn something about writing and, perhaps most important, you will learn something about yourself as a writer.

When you're thinking about what you want to write, and what kinds of things you want to write about, look at what you want to get out of your writing. We've mentioned recognition, money, and college ambitions—the reasons your parents are most likely to encourage you, perhaps—but there are also purely personal, artistic reasons to write and try to get published. Maybe you simply like to be creative. Some types of writing—fiction and poetry in particular—lend themselves to creative thought and expression. Others—nonfiction, especially journalism—use imaginative ways to write about true events. Both fiction and nonfiction can be creative, of course, and there's a big gray area between the two extremes. You can write a fictional story set against something that really happened—historical fiction. Or you can use a nonfiction style to describe fictional events.

Let's talk a little bit about the different types of writing, and the kind (or kinds) of writing you might want to do. Most writers like to try different things. Journalists often moonlight writing novels. Many novelists dabble in poetry. And it seems like many writers believe that they could write science fiction or romance novels if they felt like it. That's rarely true; both of those are distinct, strict disciplines, and writers who don't know or can't follow the form—and most of us don't and can't—end up looking silly when they try to write science fiction or romance. Indeed, each genre has its own structure. Some are more disciplined than others; some are harder for teens to break into than others. While it's tempting to try to revolutionize a certain form—"I'm going to write a book that breaks down the confining traditional structure of the novel"—you're better off getting to know the genre and the framework first. If your work doesn't conform, it may be unclassifiable and hard to sell. You have to be a really, really good writer to get unconventional work published.

In some genres, such as screenwriting, there's an accepted format that everyone uses, and there are even software programs that help you format screenplays into the accepted form.

No matter what you write, don't let your haste to submit something lead you to mark yourself as an amateur by not presenting your work in the form that editors and readers expect. Everything you submit should be technically perfect: no grammar, punctuation, or spelling mistakes, and no typos. Even if your work is technically flawless and professionally presented, however, the odds are still against it getting published. And some genres are more difficult than others. Poetry and children's books, for example, are both hard to break into not only because of the expectations that editors have, but also because so many people want to write in those genres. (This has always mystified many professional writers: children's books and poetry are among the poorest-paying work that a writer can undertake, yet those fields seem to attract the greatest number of writers, especially first-time would-be authors. On the other hand, it makes sense: if wannabes are flooding the market, the pay for poetry and children's books stays low. It's supply and demand.) A poetry book or children's book can't be merely nice or simply good. It has to be great—and that often means being different. It's an odd tension, and it applies in virtually every type of writing. Whatever we write has to conform to the rules and forms of the genre in which we are writing; it has to be familiar to readers and editors, and meet their expectations for the form. At the same time, it has to be different and fresh and surprising in the content and/or story. Whatever you write, be prepared for rejections . . . and more rejections.

On the other hand, the market for young-adult type books is filled with opportunities. Most of them are written by adults, so just by being young you're bringing something new to the genre. There's also the confessional, true-life story, either in journal form or as a memoir, which is popular right now. (See our profile of Zoe Trope on page 32.) Adults and teens alike are interested in these stories, especially true-life accounts like Zoe's description of the early years of high school. Think about other possibilities for true-life narratives by kids: a marching band or soccer season; a year as a volunteer; a summer as a camp counselor; what it's like working in an upscale bridal boutique (Tim has been trying to get Lizzie to write about that; she's got some great stories from her part-time job at Gabrielle's Bridal Suite in Ridgewood).

Comic books and graphic novels have also traditionally been marketed toward kids and teenagers—but are not usually written by them. This is a great opportunity for the artistically inclined teen to combine talents for drawing and storytelling. A number of Lizzie's friends have made their publishing debuts on web sites, sometimes their own, writing about music they like. They review popular releases, write about performances of local bands, and report the latest gossip about who's leaving which band, who's starting a band, and who's playing where or recording when. Beauty and fashion are other topics that are of interest not only to the teenagers writing and reading about teen fashions, but also to adults who are always eager for glimpses into their kids' world. One of Lizzie's first "High School Beat" columns for the weekly *Ridgewood News* was about how different groups of kids—and individuals—dress to reflect their attitude and outlook.

If you're interested in sports, especially at the local level, it's easy to get clips by writing up youth athletic events for your local paper. It's a win-win situation: teams that wouldn't otherwise get press are in the news, and you get a byline—and maybe even a check. One of Tim's best friends in the American Society of Journalists and Authors is Jim Morrison (no relation to the singer of the Doors rock group), a successful freelance writer who now lives in Virginia but grew up in the coal-mining country of Pennsylvania. As a kid, Jim was an athlete who also wrote. The local newspaper's sports editor noticed his work in his school paper. By the time he was sixteen, Morrison had a part-time job at the local paper covering minor sporting events, including some of the summer baseball leagues he played in. It wasn't unusual for him to play in a game, then come in to the newspaper office and sit down and write his story, still in his cleats and dusty uniform. Since his brief stories didn't carry a byline, he could sometimes write something like, "Jim Morrison's two-run double in the seventh inning led his team to victory. . . ." Morrison's experience also shows how kids working on the edges of adult journalism can find themselves suddenly in the middle of the mix. For instance, when the sports editor at Morrison's newspaper decided he needed a story on Muhammad Ali, who was training for a fight at his camp in Pennsylvania, and all the other "grownup" sportswriters were occupied, Morrison raised his hand and got the assignment. The boxing legend was the first of many famous people Morrison has met and interviewed over the years.

Sometimes, of course, your format and style are determined by what you're writing about. Some "little" stories are more suited to magazines or newspapers than books. Sometimes you hear a story about something and say to yourself, "Wow, that would make a great movie." You know that if you're reviewing a new music release, you literally can't write a book about it. And if you're going to write a book, you need to have enough material to fill all those pages—and make every one of them interesting. When you've found a style or genre or form of writing (or two, or five) that you're interested in, try to get as much exposure to it as possible. Go to the library and thumb through magazines and take out books to familiarize yourself with the type of work that gets published. Who writes it? How do they write it? How long is it? What kind of news and views are they presenting? What do readers get out of it? And, most important, how can *you* write about it better than anyone else? Remember, people read because it benefits them somehow. It provides them with information or inspiration. It entertains or amuses. Your job as a writer is to add value to readers' lives— and your own.

A SIMPLE MENTAL EXERCISE

If you're thinking you might like to be a published writer someday, here's a little exercise we've adapted from Sally Wendkos Olds, a prominent freelance writer (see her "Tips from a Pro" on page 120) who uses a similar version when speaking to high school students about writing. You can do in a few minutes to give you some ideas and maybe some inspiration. All you need is pen and paper.

First, at the top write down your name and the date. Then write, "By writing, I hope to . . ." and then complete the sentence. Maybe you want to get published in your local paper. Maybe you want to earn money for a new computer. Maybe you want to write a book someday. Whatever it is, however many hopes you have for your writing, jot them down.

Next, write, "The time of day I work the best is . . ." and complete the sentence. Then, "Places I'd like to write about include . . ." and finish the sentence. List as many places, general or specific, as you like.

Then list one or more books or stories you wish you had written. "I wish I had written . . ."

Next, "I want to study . . ." It doesn't have to be your prospective major in college; it can be anything you'd like to know more about.

"I feel strongly about . . ." is next, and this can be a cause, a conflict, a belief, or anything else about which you are passionate.

Then, "Three things I would like to do . . ." might be anything from spending more time with friends to traveling to outer space someday.

And finally, name a person and describe why you'd like to write about him or her. It can be someone famous or not, important or not, good or bad, alive or dead, a specific name (Mary-Kate and Ashley or Johnny Depp, for example) or a general description (the director general of the United Nations or whoever invented baseball, for example).

When you've finished, take a look at what you've written. You're holding in your hand a blueprint for becoming a published writer. Save it, and look at it when you need inspiration or a jump-start. Update it every year or so. Staying connected to what interests you can be an invaluable guide for any writer.

Christopher Paolini

Growing up in Montana, Christopher Paolini often found himself daydreaming when he was supposed to be doing his homework. When he was fifteen, he started writing down some of his daydreams about a mystical land that he called Alagaesia. It took him a year to produce the 500-page manuscript for the fantasy novel he called *Eragon* that his parents helped him self-publish.

Paolini sold several thousand copies of the book, and then a major New York publisher, Alfred A. Knopf, offered him a contract to publish and distribute *Eragon* and two other books in a trilogy about his hero, a boy who finds a magic stone that turns him into a dragon seeking revenge and liberation from the tyrant who has enslaved Alagaesia. Knopf printed 300,000 copies in 2002 when Paolini was eighteen, and the book soared onto the *New York Times* best-seller list. A movie deal followed.

Paolini, whose fresh-faced looks and eyeglasses make him look a little like Harry Potter, decided to put off college until after finishing the second and third books. When not writing he travels the country, often appearing at schools to talk about his books and about how kids can write their own stories. When students ask him how much money he is making, he just smiles and says, "My family will have food on the table for many years to come."

And when he leaves his student audiences, he offers them a kind of writers' blessing: "May your words be sharp."

. 3 .

IDEAS:
Subjects to Write About

T IM ONCE APPROACHED a magazine editor and asked her for an assignment. He began telling her about his work, and things he'd written. He wanted to assure the editor that he was a competent writer. The editor interrupted him. "Look, I'm sure you're very good writer. But so what?" she said. "Look around. There are good writers everywhere. What I need are good ideas. Bring me some ideas and we'll talk."

Ideas are the currency of writing. They're our natural resources, the vehicles for our writing. Ideas are the basis for the stories we tell. When you get right down to it, what matters are the ideas we come up with, and the stories that are inspired by those ideas.

When Tim teaches about story ideas in his writing and reporting classes at Columbia University's Graduate School of Journalism, he tells his students to "pick the low-hanging fruit." It's advice that all writers can use. Good ideas are the basis of good writing, and if you know how to look for them, they can be easy to find. Sometimes they're right in your own backyard.

A teenager's daily life is ripe with fresh story ideas. Start at school: Are there new classes? Teachers? Policies? Students? Of course, it doesn't have to be new to be a story. You could find an interesting twist, or simply a new angle of an ongoing issue. If you have a part-time job, you can write about it. Even if you aren't personally involved in something, it's still an opportunity to report on a trend or phenomenon. For instance, a lot of Lizzie's friends get summer jobs scooping ice cream. She could interview a few of them and compare their experiences working at Ben & Jerry's, Häagen-Dazs, and Van Dyk's, the local family-owned place. Or she could do her own taste-test comparison among the three. It's not hard news, but it could probably get printed in our local paper. Imagine the headline: SUMMER IS BATTLE SEASON FOR THE ICE CREAM WARS.

Journalists are taught to count, "One, two, trend." When Lizzie wrote the "High School Beat" column for the *Ridgewood News*, trends were a never-ending source of column ideas. She observed what kids wore, how they felt, how they acted, what they said, where they hung out, etc.–and then she wrote about it. Even though Lizzie was writing mostly about teenagers and the high school community, lots of parents and other adults read her columns, too. She, like all young writers who write about other kids, had the special advantage of being part of the group she was describing. Adults, especially parents, love to read about teenagers, and even though lots of grown-ups write about teens, they have a different perspective.

With this "kid's-eye view," you can write about your own experiences as well as other teens'. Unusual events—your first skydive, competing in a spelling bee—as well as normal ones described insightfully can make for great stories. If you're observant, you'll see them. Or hear about them (don't feel like you have to come up with every story idea on your own). Lots of times, you'll overhear people talking about an issue and realize that it would be an interesting subject to write about. If people are discussing it, they probably want to know more—and with some research, you can write that story.

Listening, though an important skill, is sometimes overlooked. When you're working on an idea, no matter how developed you think it is, it almost always helps to brainstorm a little bit more with other people. Their perspectives will help you present a more balanced piece of writing, rather than being totally you-centric.

Lizzie loves this approach. Before sitting down to write her "High School Beat" columns, she'd discuss the week's topic with friends and family alike. In addition to getting other people's ideas on an issue, it helps her articulate her own views. Like Lizzie, you might find that it's sometimes easier to express yourself out loud rather than on a piece of paper. Once you've developed your ideas in conversation, you can more easily write them down.

You can also get ideas from the newspaper. Yes, the "news" has already been reported, but there's often a story behind the one in the paper. Last May, we saw a short article in *The New York Times* about a group of Westchester County, New York, teenagers who were having a drinking party and locked themselves in the house when the cops came to break it up. The standoff between kids and local police lasted for almost three hours and only ended when parents started showing up at the house and threatening summer-long groundings. A number of people we know, both kids and adults, talked about the story for a few days, mostly, "How could those kids be so crazy?" and then it kind of disappeared. About a week later, though, *New York* magazine ran a minute-by-minute, 4,000-word feature on the night's events. It was a great idea—people who had seen the blurb in the *Times* remembered the story and wanted to hear more. The story was also able to reach, and intrigue, a much wider audience on the cover of a magazine than when it had been buried in the *Times'* Metro section. Because the piece in *New York* was more personal and included the teens' side of the story, it added welcome depth to an article that had already been written.

You only need a different perspective to make this kind of story work. It could be more focused on your own community—for instance, how federal budget cuts will affect your town's schools—or even on a certain person, like a new teacher.

Focus on what interests you. A fascinating subject makes a story easier to write, read, and ultimately sell. One classic idea is a profile of an extraordinary person in ordinary circumstances, or an ordinary person in extraordinary circumstances.

It's that dose of the unexpected that keeps readers captivated. Look for people with special talents or cool hobbies—even if you don't end up writing about them, they can open your eyes to other good story ideas.

Other ways of life, especially how other teenagers live, is another good topic to keep in mind. One year when Tim had a lot of magazine assignments in different parts of the world, he came up with an idea: What do teenagers around the world think of America and Americans? He pitched the idea to *Seventeen* magazine, which loved it. Over the next few months, wherever he went—Russia, England, France, Hong Kong, China, and elsewhere—he found teenagers and interviewed them. That story about teenagers around the world led him to another good idea for *Seventeen*: profiles of three 17-year-old girls growing up in different parts of the country. One was a city kid in Manhattan, another a farm girl in Illinois, and the third was growing up in the suburbs of Mill Valley in northern California. What was great about that story was not so much the differences between the girls—the city girl would go clubbing on weekends, while the farm girl went to keggers in the woods—but about their similarities: the shared hopes, dreams, fears, and uncertainties that are part of growing up for everybody.

Some people like to think of strangers as friends they haven't met yet. We like to think of them as stories we haven't written yet. After all, people are what stories are really about. And you can find those people everywhere. But you need to be looking for them, and to be open and receptive to people. For instance, people you meet at airports, in restaurants, or when you're traveling can offer insights about the world that you—

and other people where you're from—haven't considered. Of course, you won't always agree, but provocative opinions and quotes can form the basis of a thoughtful piece of writing.

In many ways, coming up with ideas is the hard part. After you've found some, don't let them slip out of your memory. Even if you think you'll never forget the brilliant result of a late-night brainstorming session, write it down. And then remember where you wrote it. Story ideas can strike at any time, so be prepared. Try to always keep pen and paper handy for jotting down interesting thoughts or comments that may be useful later. Some of the best ideas have been scribbled on napkins or the backs of train schedules, so don't limit brainstorming to your desk. It's helpful to create a system for keeping and organizing your story ideas, whether it's a simple list on loose-leaf paper, a special section in your filing cabinet, or a program on your computer. Take those little scraps of ideas, whether scrawled on a napkin or in the margin of your notebook or on the back of your hand, and store them someplace where you'll see and remember them. Along with your own ideas, you should save newspaper and magazine clippings that might provide inspiration for future stories. Ask Sam and InfoSelect are two popular types of software that writers use to store notes and ideas. They're handier than paper-based systems because they can save electronic files, including the full text of articles from the Internet. If you have a system to organize everything, you can go back to it whenever you want, instead of trying to finish one story or perfect one idea before starting another.

Expect ideas to change form and develop and evolve. Say you're writing a straight news article on a recent blizzard for your school newspaper. Midway through your research, you meet and interview a girl who loves to snowshoe. Thanks to her unusual hobby, she enjoyed the blizzard that disrupted everyone else's routines. You could just quote her in your article, or you could change your story to make her the focus, along with other people who welcomed the blizzard because they like unconventional winter sports. Or you could file away the idea for a magazine story later on how she snowshoed around the neighborhood making sure elderly people who couldn't get out were all right. There are an infinite number of ways to interpret the situation in writing—you could decide on one, or try several of them. It all depends on your own strengths and interests as a writer.

Many idea-finding strategies are aimed at searching for news to break. However, you don't have to be (or want to be) a journalist to think this way. Writing about current, interesting topics in any format—from poetry to investigative reporting—will make the whole process more exciting and improve your chances of getting published. Consider what people are interested in knowing more about. Think about what *you* are interested in knowing more about. If you want to know more about something, it's probably something that other people would want to know more about, and it's probably a story.

Remember, people—readers, editors, everybody—don't really care about whether you're a good writer. They care about the stories you tell. Think about it this way. When you read something you like in a newspaper or magazine, you typically say, "Whoa, that was a good story." You don't say, "Whoa, this is a good writer." Writers are only as good as the stories they tell.

Really, that's what we are: storytellers. So make sure you work hard to find the best ideas, and learn to shape them and focus them in order to tell the story in the best way for the readers you are trying to reach.

• A GLANCE AT A YOUNG WRITER •

Zoe Trope

Zoe Trope isn't her real name, but then again, Zoe Trope isn't your average teenager. She's also a published author who got a fat advance from a major publishing house. Her memoir, *Please Don't Kill the Freshman,* came out when she was sixteen and already a high school graduate—she completed the graduation requirements in three years at her Portland, Oregon, high school.

Writing comes naturally to Zoe, who explained, "I got read to a lot as a child, so I read a lot . . . that lends itself to writing." In middle school, she remembered, "I'd stay in from recess to type stories on the teacher's computer. The teacher never took us to the computer lab, so that was the only time I had to write." Despite her literary leanings, she never actually considered writing as a potential career. To her, the prospect of getting published "was always a very faraway, intangible thing, like a nice car that would be nice to own. But you don't go out and get a job and save up to buy it right then."

The turning point came for Zoe in an after-school writing class she took in eighth grade. Kevin Sampsell, a writer and events coordinator at Powell's, a bookstore in Portland, taught the class. Sampsell's approach was unconventional, but it ignited Zoe's imagination. His focus on edgy styles of writing, like flash fiction (quick "snapshots" of a situation or dialogue), helped her realize that "I could write whatever I wanted to—it didn't have to fit linear, traditional definitions of writing."

After the class ended, Zoe continued to correspond with Sampsell by e-mail. He'd recommend obscure books for her to read and bands for her to listen to, and she would share some of her journal entries about life as a freshman in high school. Sampsell, recognizing the potential of Zoe's wit and insights about herself and her peers, helped her collect some of the entries and publish them as a chapbook of stories under his own imprint, Future Tense Press. The chapbook was only about thirteen thousand words long, photocopied and stapled together, but it sold well at Powell's and other local bookstores. "People liked it," Zoe said, noting that her chapbook had a print run of three thousand copies, even though the standard print run of chapbooks is only a few hundred copies.

Eventually, Sampsell passed the chapbook along through acquaintances to a literary agent in New York. The agent loved *Please Don't Kill the Freshman* and contacted Zoe about expanding it for possible sale to a publishing house. At first, she resisted—"I got scared, basically"—and refused to edit the diary. However, with some prodding from Sampsell she changed her mind and got a six-figure book deal with HarperCollins. In October of 2003, *PDKTF* came out on HarperCollins' young-adult imprint, HarperTempest. The original chapbook became the first section of the book, supplemented by more journal entries from her freshman and sophomore years of high school.

Since then, some parts of Zoe's life have changed and others have remained the same. She's still a teenager, hanging out with her friends, writing in her blog (www.zoe-trope.com) and getting ready to go to college. But now she's a published author. Everyone who knows her knows about the book, but "it's not as weird as you might think," she said. Her friends, identified in the book by code names like Linux Shoe and Vegan Grrl, "have been supportive . . . they're still excited about it," she said, even though her descriptions of them in the book weren't always glowing with praise.

The book's subject matter, running from mundane (Zoe's bored in school, she hates standardized tests, she wants to buy a car) to the provocative (Zoe and her friends dealing with sex, drinking, drugs, and disillusionment) probably won't shock teen readers, but it might alarm their parents. However, while acknowledging that some of the material is "very controversial," Zoe says that she hasn't encountered many negative reactions. "It's sweet, everyone's really happy and proud. What's in there is some version of the truth as I saw it at the time. Yeah, it's my life. I'm not embarrassed. If it was anything someone didn't know, they probably wouldn't be surprised."

She also enjoyed the benefits that go along with getting a book deal at the age of fifteen, including the money. She was shocked at the taxes, but there was enough left over for a new laptop, her first trip to New York, some college savings, and, yes, a used car. She's also become a minor Portland celebrity, giving readings and book signings alongside older, more established authors. In fact, one of the things she relishes most about being an author is getting to meet her favorite writers, including Dave Eggers and

Chuck Palahnuik. "Being published," Zoe added, "your name come up for other projects," like a recent anthology called *Sixteen* to which she contributed a short story.

When Lizzie talked to her, Zoe had started working on another book, a novel this time, which she'll most likely end up writing in college. "I write every day, one way or another," she said, whether it's in e-mails or on her LiveJournal, but progress on the book is slow. For her to write productively, she said, "My brain has to be really full, then I empty all of it out . . . I don't deal well with people snapping their fingers and telling me to do stuff now." Spoken like a true teenager.

Lizzie Says:
DON'T GET TOO PERSONAL

Not every writer wants to get as personal as Zoe Trope. I don't. In the "High School Beat" column I wrote for our local paper, I tried to keep the subject matter interesting for students as well as their parents, and even Ridgewood residents who had no connection to the local high school. For example, in one column in the fall of my senior year about the stresses of the college application process, I avoided getting into the specifics of my own college choices, transcript, SAT scores, and grade point average. Most readers don't really care about that stuff, and if they do, it's none of their business.

Instead, I wrote about how easy it is to ignore the simple pleasures of life when it feels like everything you do is focused on gaining the approval of the First Choice College.

I got a lot of positive feedback on that column after it ran in the local weekly, so I sold a shorter version to the Bergen County (N.J.) *Record,* a larger regional paper. I had known that more people would read it in the *Record,* but it was still a surprise when I walked into English class the morning after my article ran and my teacher was passing out copies to the class. A friend later told me that another English teacher–one who didn't know me at all–had done the same thing, except he also had held a class discussion on my piece and encouraged his students to write their own essays about applying to college.

. 4 .

MARKETS:
Who Will Publish You?

W E'VE TALKED ABOUT finding ideas, topics, and subjects. And we've looked at research and writing. But we
also need to talk about where we can get published—and how
that influences our choices when we are deciding what to write
about. Writers tend to call the places that publish their work
"markets," and in the next few chapters we'll look at the various
types of markets, including the school newspaper, which is the
first market for many young writers. We'll also discuss bigger
"traditional" markets: primarily general-circulation newspapers, magazines, and books. And we'll examine the many opportunities afforded by so-called "new" media, which are for

the most part online or digital markets. There are advantages and disadvantages to both traditional markets and new media for the young writer, and it inevitably pays to know something about the market before you try to "pitch" (that's writer talk for submissions and queries) your writing to an editor—and often before you decide what to write about.

Before we get into specifics, let's think about markets in general. Most writers, from the best-selling author to the kid staring at a blank screen before making his or her first blog entry, is faced with a very big choice: Should you write about what you want to write about, or should you write what people want to read? Another way of looking at it: Do you write for the sake of writing, for the art of it? Or do you write what will get you recognition and maybe money? The most fortunate writers manage to do both. They write about topics they want to write about, and write about them in the style they like. For the rest of us, for most writers, the choice is simple; if we want to get published, if we want recognition and rewards, we write what people want to read. We write what the markets will print. Obviously, without markets we couldn't get published. That puts enormous power in the hands of editors, the people who make the decisions for those markets about what gets published and what doesn't. We need them. But look at it the other way, too. Without writers, the markets wouldn't have anything to publish. They wouldn't exist. They need a constant stream of new ideas, new stories, and new writers. They need us as much as much as we need them.

In this chapter we'll look at the "youth" markets in so-called traditional media—print, primarily—and the various ways teen writers can break in, especially at newspapers. Magazines don't publish as often or have as much space for stories, so it's natural that newspapers, with more need for editorial copy, are a better potential market for writers who want to get into print.

For many young writers, the first market for their work is the school newspaper. If you haven't considered this, or haven't tried it yet, we recommend it. The worst that happens is you do it for a semester or two and quit. The best that happens is you love it, make friends, learn a lot, and become known at your school (and beyond, sometimes) as a good writer. If you stick with it you might become editor of a section, and eventually editor-in-chief—and that's a huge arrow in your quiver when it comes time to apply for colleges. Admissions counselors at many schools give being editor of a high school newspaper the same weight on applications as being captain of a varsity team or president of your class. There are some downsides, of course. Writing about school issues and events can get monotonous. Other students serving as editors can be bossy and demanding and unreasonable. (Many adult professional writers say that doesn't change just because editors grow up.) The clips are less impressive than a "real" newspaper, and of course there's no pay. But there can be huge benefits in what you learn and take with you to bigger and better writing gigs—and that's the real point of working on a school paper.

At the beginning of Lizzie's junior year in high school, she joined the school paper, the *High Times,* as a staff photographer. It was her first school paper position since a stint as coeditor of the Ridge School *Raccoon* in fifth grade, and considerably more productive. Within a few months she realized that photography, while a fun hobby, was not her journalistic strength and she quickly switched over to writing. Looking back, it probably had something to do with her complete inability to shoot decent sports photos. But she could write better-than-decent sports articles, so it was writing from then on.

Some people thrive on pressure and adversity. In high school, Lizzie found, those people work on the school paper. There was a lot of big news during her two years at the *High Times,* most of it bad—school budget cuts, a barely averted teachers' strike, and the departures of many valued, experienced teachers and administrators. She and her colleagues covered it all, usually in a frenzied rush for interviews, photos, edits, and re-edits, even though by the time the paper actually came out its news would generally be outdated.

There were benefits, too. In Lizzie's case, she got practical experience writing on deadline—and gained the confidence that she could write under pressure—as well as the feeling of accomplishment that every writer feels at seeing his or her byline on the front page. In her senior year, serving as news editor and entertainment editor, Lizzie also got her first taste of what it's like to edit the work of her peers, many of whom were also close friends. "It's really interesting," she'd tell Tim after a long evening of laying out the paper, "how you interact with your friends when you're working within this hierarchy. I'm an editor, below the editors-in-chief but above the writers, and sometimes it's weird telling them what to do, or being told what to do."

As most teens' first step into the world of writing and journalism, school papers are similar to real life in that once you're on the staff of a newspaper, you get regular assignments from the same editor (or editors), but also different because most teen writers don't go straight into newspaper jobs. Instead, it's more common for a kid to start off like a freelancer, submitting individual pieces to different publications in the hopes of getting published. Working on a school paper offers a valuable glimpse into what it's like in a real newsroom—where you could eventually end up if you stick with journalism.

If you're interested in getting involved with your own school paper, the time to do it is at the beginning of the year. On the *High Times,* that's when they recruited staff writers and artists. Even if you're not sure whether you really want to do it, or you have a fall sport or activity that keeps you busy for the first few months of school, go to the introductory meetings anyway and get your name on their list. That way, if you decide to get involved later on or suddenly have enough free time to participate in the middle of the year, you won't be some random kid who walks in.

From Lizzie's experience on the *High Times,* there were always too many staffers at the beginning of the year and way too few at the end. Volunteer writers in, say, April were much more valuable (and much rarer) than the same people who volunteered in September—so be persistent. If you think working on the school paper might be fun but you don't get any assignments in the fall, try back a few months later. Once things settle down, your help might be much more gratefully received.

Another appealing option for novice writers is the local paper. The daily newspapers in many small- to medium-size communities are receptive to receiving story submissions from teens—and from anybody else. And in both big cities and small towns there are often weekly newspapers that welcome teens' submissions. Any publication that focuses on community events is a worthy target. Some papers, including large ones that would be difficult for kids to break into otherwise, have special kid or teen sections that feature writing by young people.

Our local weekly, the *Ridgewood News*, started up its own student section, called "Our Voices," in March of 2003. The editors' original vision for "Our Voices" has changed since then; in the first meetings to plan the section, they wanted lots of teen-related news and opinion pieces. But now it's evolved to mostly entertainment news, movie and concert reviews, and some book report essays. That's the thing about publications that don't assign articles or pay for them; they become more like forums. They have to take whatever people submit, and people who aren't being assigned or paid are going to write "easy" stuff. Look at it this way. Suppose the editor would love to get an in-depth analysis of what kids think about the budget cuts that are going to hurt the school's arts program, but the editor can't pay even a few bucks for the story. Instead, the editor gets five reviews of the latest blockbuster movie. The contributors are simply picking the low-hanging fruit. If they were getting paid even a few dollars, they'd probably reach higher for rarer, better fruit. On the other hand, without a lot of hard news in "Our Voices," there's more room for kids' creative work, like poetry and short stories, even though it's not the usual territory covered in a weekly paper. Our local paper also runs a column, shared by three high school students, called "High School Beat" that covers, naturally enough, the high school.

Lizzie was a "High School Beat" columnist for most of her last two years in high school. Generally it was a great experience, even though she wishes it had ended differently. Let's have Tim step aside and let Lizzie tell you about it in her own words:

"Up until the spring of 2003, our local paper, the *Ridgewood News*, had only one student-penned regular feature—the 'High School Beat' column. Along with two other Ridgewood High School students, I was a columnist during my junior and senior years. The three of us rotated columns, so I was responsible for one approximately eight hundred-word piece on high school life every three weeks. We had a lot of latitude in terms of subjects. Pretty much anything directly or indirectly connected to teens or RHS was fair game. I wrote one early column about whether it's possible to have too much self-esteem, and the next on students' political activism in the run-up to the war in Iraq.

"Then the *Ridgewood News* decided to expand its capacity for student writing by starting 'Our Voices,' a tabloid pullout section dedicated to articles, reviews, opinion pieces, and art by middle and high schoolers. They held a meeting to form a core base of writers; the 'High School Beat' columnists were invited, as well as a few of our friends, and some other good writers who'd been recommended by English teachers in the Ridgewood schools.

"We were all pretty excited about the idea of having our own section of the paper to write for—and nearly unlimited freedom in terms of stories—until the final issue came up: money. It had never been the *Ridgewood News*'s policy to pay 'High School Beat' writers, but I had assumed that there would be at least token payments for regular contributors to what amounted to a mini-paper for kids. But no. The editors made it clear that they expected to receive news, opinions and editorials, entertainment features, a wide range of reviews, and sports stories, plus photos to illustrate the whole thing, every week of the school year—and all without paying a nickel for them. All they offered us in return for our work were clips that they said would enhance our resumes and college applications. Now, clips are great. There's no question in my mind that copies of my work, from both the *Ridgewood News* and elsewhere, helped me get into college. But in my mind, that was a fair trade-off. (Plus, I was paid one hundred dollars each for the *Record* articles—but more later on bigger markets and getting paid.)

"To me, the amount of work the editors wanted from our initially small group was just too much to justify being compensated only in clips. 'Our "Voices" would make money for the paper from the advertisements in its pages—why shouldn't writers receive even a small amount in return for their work? Because we didn't feel like we were getting adequately compensated, most of the high school recruits didn't submit much to 'Our Voices.' A few of my friends wrote some short news pieces, and I reworked and submitted an article I'd already written for the *High Times* on RHS's new policy banning peanut products from being sold in the cafeteria.

"Gradually, submissions from my friends and other high schoolers to 'Our Voices' seemed to dwindle. The writing published in the section was mostly from middle schoolers, and as I saw it, of a lower quality than the editors had originally hoped for. When they decided to move the 'High School Beat' column over to 'Our Voices,' presumably to help fill the section and raise the quality of the writing, I objected. The column had lots of adult readers, ones who knew me and ones who didn't, and I didn't think it was right to use it to jump-start the faltering kids' section. I asked that the column, at least when I would write it, continue to be displayed in the usual 'adult' pages where adults expected to find it, rather than in the kids' section that I knew many adults didn't read (because they told me so). The editors said the column had to run in 'Our Voices,' which was by then written almost exclusively by middle-schoolers, so I found a replacement writer to finish up my portion of the remaining columns in the second semester of my senior year. I had enjoyed writing the column, but I didn't want to demean my work by continuing it under those circumstances."

Fortunately, the editors at the *Ridgewood News* respected Lizzie's decision—we're sure they wished their parent company would agree to pay young writers—and they remained friendly to her. Whether young writers get paid or not, local newspapers can be a great way to break into print, and one clip from a "real" newspaper has more credibility and is more impressive on a resume than a dozen clips from a student newspaper. A number of other newspapers around the country, both weekly and daily, have their own versions of a section for teen writers. For example, larger papers such as the *Denver Post, Sacramento Bee,* and *Providence Journal* regularly feature kids' work in a special page or section. In Boston, there's even a quarterly paper devoted to teens' writing. It's called TiP—Teens in Print—and it was created in the summer of 2003 by *The Boston Globe* and WriteBoston, an initiative promoting writing in Boston's schools. Like most other teen writing outlets, it accepts nonfiction as well as fiction submissions. And some teen sections do pay for articles.

One of the best teen sections is in Pennsylvania; it's the "Voices" section of the *Reading Eagle*. It's notable both for its longevity—next year will be its tenth—and for the fact that it pays its contributors for their work. Twice a year, editors take applications from high school students all over Berks County who want to join the writing staff. Once accepted, writers contribute once or twice a month, either in the newspaper or on the "Voices" Web site. The pay per piece is between $10 and $25, left to the editor's discretion. Rather than focusing on hard news, the editors encourage the teens to write about their interests and what's going on in their lives. On the "Voices" Web site, this approach translates into interactive quizzes and bulletin boards along with

reviews and commentary–check out http://voices.reading
eagle.com/.

LISA SCHEID Q&A

Lisa Scheid, the editor of "Voices" at the *Reading Eagle*, one of
the best newspaper sections we found that is written for and by
teenagers, answered some questions from Lizzie:

Q. *How much do "Voices" writers get paid?*

A. We have a sliding scale of $10 to $25 per published piece.
Each writer gets a rubric of what we expect for $25. The
pay is at the editor's discretion. At the request of our teen
executive board a few years ago, we pay $25 for only the
very best pieces.

Q. *Where does the money come from?*

A. The newspaper's budget. Technically, it is the editorial department. There are ads sold for "Voices," but the revenue hardly
supports the pay of two veteran journalists running the section, let alone pay for the teens. This is really a commitment
the paper has to the community and to its future readers and
journalists. We are locally owned and I'm very proud of the
publisher's interest in teens. Next year is our tenth anniversary and I'm hoping to study how the section has impacted
the hundreds of teens who have written for it over the years.

Q. *We're also interested in the types of kids who work for the section. You take new applicants twice a year, but how does the application process work? Are writers ever taken off the "Voices" staff? Why?*

A. We get all types of kids, with different interests, high school social groups (preps, jocks etc.) and abilities. I'm really proud of that and want to make sure we keep it that way. They must be in ninth to twelfth grade and live in Berks County. We ask applicants to send us a 200-word critique of the section. We want it to be honest, not a kiss-up. The criticism helps the editors understand our audience better. The application gives us an idea of a student's writing ability but we haven't rejected anyone yet. I'm proud of that, too. That leaves us with a large roster so students tend to get just a story or two a month. We have a strike system in which a writer who misses an unexcused deadline gets a strike. Three strikes and you are out for three months. If it happens again, you are gone for good. That has never happened as far as I know. I'm pretty lenient and I have backup stories. I'm lenient when a writer has a good reason to be late—problems with sources is an example. Re-write is another reason. We view "Voices" as part professional publication, part learning experience. I know of only one teen who was "let go" and that was due to plagiarism. After teens are accepted they are required to attend an introductory session on journalism. We also give workshops each month for those who are really interested.

Q. *What do you look for in submissions? What kinds of work get rejected? How often does the average writer actually get published?*

A. The work published in "Voices" has a wide range. I don't outright reject work. Usually, I send it back for a rewrite or more reporting. Kids get published maybe once or twice a month either in the newspaper or on our Web site, which has some exclusive content.

Q. *Are there some common mistakes (in writing, reporting) that kids tend to make?*

A. As for mistakes, the one thing that bugs me the most in teen journalism is lack of attribution and generalized statements—"Many teens think," or statements like that. You could probably make a case that it goes on in mainstream journalism as well but I can only talk about my corner of the world. Also poor usage, which is embarrassing to the writer: *then* for *than*, things like that. But I can fix that; I can't fix lack of reporting.

Q. *Do you have a favorite type of article?*

A. My favorite pieces are personal stories . . . a visit to the Holocaust museum, a vegetarian learning to fish, a girl realizing her noble grandfather has Alzheimer's, hanging with friends on a moonlit night, being in a car crash. Teens are well suited to write these.

Lizzie Says:
WRITING A COLUMN

Like pretty much anything else, writing a column has upsides and not-so-upsides. I wrote a column called "High School Beat" in our local paper, the *Ridgewood News*, for about a year and a half. The column ran every week, but there were three of us who shared writing it, so I actually only had to write one column every third week. Approximately eight hundred words every three weeks—not so bad, right? In theory.

When I first started as a columnist, I managed my time pretty well. Of my three weeks per column, I budgeted the first to do nothing. My mind-set was, why worry about something that's not due for almost a month? During the second week, I'd look for ideas. Sometimes this meant combing through the newspaper for current events I could link to high school events; other times I just talked to friends, teachers, and acquaintances about what was going on in school. When it got down to the last week, I started writing. Okay, usually it was the weekend before the column was due before I actually sat down at the computer to write. Sunday afternoon of that last weekend, to be exact.

On occasion, my tendency to procrastinate was an asset. March of my junior year comes to mind—every time

I tried to brainstorm ideas for my upcoming column, I could only think about how much I despised the month of March. I always have. Where we live, at least, March is the muddy in-between stage after winter and before spring. What cool or interesting things could I possibly write about? In desperation, I pulled out the school's calendar and made a list of all the month's events, including the school drama company's annual musical, varsity basketball championships, and, of course, St. Patrick's Day. Then I used my list to compile an unconventional column: the Top 10 Reasons to Like (or just not hate) March. Numbers ten through two were fun March activities or facts, and number one was—what else?—the fact that only thirty-one days were left until the beginning of April.

A big part of the job was finding new angles on high school life. As much as I put off writing the columns, once I had a good idea the writing came easily. Doing columns was like any other type of writing: good ideas mean good pieces. When I first started, the hardest thing for me— harder than managing my time or meeting deadlines—was knowing where to look for ideas and, once I'd gotten a few good ones, how to refine them for my purpose. Eventually, I realized that column ideas were everywhere. Was a big school event coming up? Had something controversial or newsworthy happened recently? Even seasonal topics could be spun into columns—holiday gift-giving etiquette among teens, or the "senioritis" that strikes students in every grade each spring.

One thing that surprised me when I first started writing "High School Beat" was the scope of my audience. I had assumed that mostly kids would read it, but many more parents than kids told me they'd seen my columns. Once I figured that out, I tried to broaden my subjects a little bit so they'd be interesting for adults as well as students of all ages. I'd never realized before how many people were interested in the lives of high school students.

SAMPLE COLUMN:
"Which College? Don't Ask"

WHICH COLLEGE? DON'T ASK
By Lizzie Harper
"High School Beat," Ridgewood News, *May 2, 2003*

Spending spring break looking at colleges is, I guess, a rite of passage for Ridgewood High School juniors. It's when you pack up and schlep around to ten colleges in as many days, trying to decide where you want to spend what everyone says are the "best" years of your life. This decision is highly un-scientific, based mostly on how a few students are dressed, the weather on the day of your visit, and people you know who go there.

At least, that's how I go about deciding if I like a school or not. My college-visiting trip last week went by in a blur of bad food and enthusiastic tour guides. At every school there was a little card to fill out, an uncomfortable couch to sit on, a library to see, and an information session to sit through. Not the most thrilling way to spend spring break.

But when I get to college it will be worth all the trouble, right? No parents, no curfew, no rules . . . No comfy bed, no home-cooked meals, no private bathroom. As much as I'm looking forward to college, there's something to be said for appreciating the comforts of home while I still have them. Of course, whatever college I end up at will become my home, but home will also be at our house in Ridgewood for as long as my parents live here. When I visited Occidental College in Los Angeles in February, my host Erica and her friends would say things like, "When I go home after dinner I should call home." To them, home is both a dorm room and a house hundreds or thousands of miles away.

I'm not going to leave home for another year and a half, but looking at colleges makes me realize how much I'll miss my home and family in Ridgewood. My mom and I saw five colleges last week, and after each visit we would discuss the school, its surroundings, and its students. These discussions often led to talking about other, completely unrelated things. Like politics. And her job, because I've never figured out exactly what it is that she does. And—life in general.

My mom and I don't get a chance to sit down and talk

very often, unless it's about when I have to come home or how long I'll be grounded if I don't clean my room. But on a long drive in a rental car, there isn't anything to do but talk—especially when the only radio station you can find is playing polka music. (One of the schools we visited was the University of Wisconsin.) I appreciated my mom's company a lot on this trip, whether she was rolling her eyes at an incompetent tour guide or telling me stories about her own college days. I loved hearing her stories, but I have a feeling she's not telling me everything. Thank goodness.

It's ironic that my mom and I bonded over something that will eventually separate us. In a year and a half, I'll be living in a dorm room while she is still here in Ridgewood. But it will be a dorm room at a school that she helped me choose. (It will also be a dorm room at a school that she and my dad will be paying an obscene amount of tuition for, but I haven't brought that up yet.) I know that home will be where my mom is, as well as where I am. In this phase of my life, when there are so many choices to make—everything from what college I attend to what I do with my life—it's comforting to know that my mom will help me. It doesn't matter how many miles are between us; we can always talk.

Next Sunday, May 11, is Mother's Day, so I want to tell her: Thanks a lot, Mom, and Happy Mother's Day. Maybe someday you'll be ready to tell me the rest of those college stories. And maybe someday I'll be ready to hear them.

NEW MEDIA:
Establishing Yourself
in Cyberspace

WITH THE RISE of the Internet, online publishing has become a huge and viable market for all writers, including teens. As with all publishing options, there are advantages and disadvantages. With a basic understanding of how it all works, though, you can get all the benefits with a minimum of difficulty.

First, figure out what kind of Web publishing you're interested in. There are many kinds, ranging from slick and professional to artsy and specialized—from big name, magazine-style sites to personal blogs you can create yourself. In between there are specialized sites, like ones that focus on writing by kids, or service/community-oriented ones that often accept kids' work. (More about those in later in this chapter.)

Going right for the big sites is shooting pretty high, but if your work (and luck) is good enough, it's possible to get published on one of them. Most, like *Salon* and *Slate,* have content and format similar to that of a magazine. There are news articles, editorials, features, columns, reviews, even comics. However, check out the site before you submit anything. Do they accept unsolicited submissions? If they do, is it only in certain departments? Without answering these questions, your hard work and writing might go to waste. For instance, *Salon*'s Life editor, Lori Leibovitch, told Lizzie that although she "rarely" accepts work by teens, she looks for "good writing and a strong point of view" in submissions. And to her, it's definitely a plus if you identify yourself as a teen writer.

Despite the similarities to traditional magazines and print media, Web sites are very different. For one thing, they're capable of holding much more content, so writing can be archived online for months, or even years. They're also updated more frequently—depending on the site, it could be more than once a day—so the traditional waiting period to see your work in print will be much shorter.

Web sites that only publish kids' work abound on the Internet, and for the writer who's just starting out, they're a more realistic goal. National Scholastic Sports and News (www.nssan. com) is one site like this that's based in our area of northern New Jersey but welcomes students—and participating schools—from anywhere. Founded by Brian Corcoran, NSSAN sets up collaborations with teachers (and sometimes pays the teachers) to edit and submit their students' best writing on school events, news, sports, entertainment, and social trends.

Another good site with plenty of writing for and by kids is Channel One. (www.channelone.com) It's the Internet branch of Channel One News, a TV news show broadcast to high schools and middle schools nationwide. On the News page, kids' writing and art contributions are featured prominently alongside new headlines from the Associated Press. In the submission guidelines, which are available on the site, would-be contributors are advised to "make your articles logical, literate, smart and creative."

There are also sites like FictionPress (www.fictionpress.com) and TeenInk (www.teenink.com) where writers can join and post work. On sites like these, the writing is often more personal and creative than what you'd see in the average school paper. It's a good place to share "writing for writing's sake"— self-directed work like essays, reviews, memoirs, and humor. On some sites, readers can review your work. It might be scary to read strangers' comments below your writing, but the constructive criticism is often helpful.

If you decide to strike out on your own in cyberspace, there's always the blog. Blogs, short for Web logs, have become increasingly popular among the Web-savvy as well as the not-so-savvy. They're easy to create and use, and offer nearly unlimited creative freedom to write whatever you want and publish it on the Web. Some of the most popular teen blogging sites are LiveJournal (www.livejournal.com), DiaryLand (www.diaryland.com), and Xanga (www.xanga.com). Everyone blogs differently; some people post a few thoughts or noteworthy activities each day, while others share longer pieces. Most blog sites also have a "comment" feature where readers can offer feedback.

Writing online, especially in a blog, can have its dangers. There's often a false sense of security or privacy on the Internet. Who's going to ever find this, you might wonder. However, it's important to keep in mind that anyone—your parents, your friends, your future employers—can read what you post. It could be as mild as criticizing a friend on your LiveJournal, but if your friend (or anyone who knows her) finds out, you'll wish you'd been more sensible.

Another side note about propriety in cyberspace involves names. Namely, what you name yourself. Your screen name and e-mail address are an important reflection of who you are; if you want to be seen as a mature, though young writer, your name should reinforce that image. For instance, PartyGirll might be fine for chatting with your friends, but would probably keep you from being taken seriously by strangers. Consider setting up a separate "writing" e-mail account (www.hotmail. com and many other sites offer free e-mail) that you can use to correspond with editors and other writers. It'll also help keep your writing business separate from personal stuff.

Finally, if you don't want to go on someone else's Web site, create your own. AOL and many other ISPs (Internet Service Providers) offer free or low-cost Web hosting; they'll let you fill up a few pages with whatever you want. One of the guys at Lizzie's school, for example, started a site that focuses on new music, and a number of her friends contributed sporadically to it during their high school years. With a Web site where they could publish their reviews, some of them were also able to do phone and e-mail interviews with musicians and singers from well-known groups. If you do set up a Web site of your own, you might want to consider investing a few dollars to get your own domain name and then have it "forward" visitors to your Web site. For example, Tim set up a Web site with a company called Netopia; his URL, technically, is www.nvo.com/ timharper. But by registering the domain name, timharper.com for a few dollars a year, and paying for forwarding for a few more dollars a year, people can use that relatively simple—and easy to remember—cyber-address to reach his Web page. Look around for the best deals—price, service, how big the site is—for Web hosting, domain names, and forwarding services.

• A GLANCE AT A YOUNG WRITER •

Stephen Yellin

About three dozen bloggers were given press credentials to the Democratic national convention in Boston during the summer of 2004. Some were journalists, but most of them were just regular people who were invited to come, observe, and write about the whole experience in their online journals.

One of them was Stephen Yellin, then sixteen, a high school student from Berkeley Heights, New Jersey. He was invited, according to *The New York Times*, because of his political observations contributed to DailyKos.com, which describes itself as "Political analysis and other daily rants on the state of the nation."

Unlike traditional journalists, Yellin and other bloggers at the

Democratic convention made it clear that they are party activists. "What bloggers do for the Democrats is that we enable the party base, those who are in the middle or upper class who are deeply involved in Internet and activism, to get a viewpoint they can get fired up about," Yellin told the *Times*.

Some bloggers raised money through their journals and Web sites to finance their trips to Boston for the convention, but Yellin didn't need to. "My parents are paying," he reported.

VOLUNTEER WRITING

There are reasons to write beyond recognition, money, and an impressive college application—community service is one. Sure, volunteering at a soup kitchen is good, but why not find a way to serve your community that uses your special skills as a teen writer?

One way to do this is by using your writing to get publicity for local service programs. Here's our own project: Tim is on the board of our county's Volunteer Center, an organization that coordinates all kinds of volunteer activities in the area, like mentoring, helping the homeless, and maintaining public parks. He's a mentor, too, so that's how we got the idea to profile mentors for local newspapers. Everyone benefits from the project—the mentors get recognized for their contributions, the Volunteer Center gets publicity, and the writer (in this case, Lizzie) gets a few clips from local papers. And if the Volunteer Center wants to, they can use the profiles on their Web site—another "clip" where you've been published.

We're still in the process of getting the project, called Mentoring Moments, into motion. The hardest part is getting in touch with mentors and finding time with them for a short interview; after that, writing an 800- to 1,000-word profile is easy. Getting them published is pretty simple, too; most community weeklies welcome articles on local go-gooders.

You can follow our example by contacting your local community service organization about possible subjects. They can provide you with lists of mentors, workers, or other people to contact. It doesn't even need to be a series; if you want, you can just write about local opportunities for community service. By writing about it, you're making your own contribution by raising awareness in the community, as well as getting valuable writing and reporting practice and maybe even some good clips—from the newspaper and maybe even a Web site—for your portfolio.

.6.

MOVING UP:
Bigger and Better Markets

Okay, you write for your school paper. You've had some of your writing posted on Web sites or published online in zines. Maybe you've had some of your work printed in the "teens" section of your local weekly or daily newspaper. That's all great. But are you satisfied? The truth is, because there are so many more opportunities for teenagers to be published these days—especially online—it's becoming more important than ever, if you want to distinguish yourself as a writer, to move on to bigger and better markets. Especially paying markets. If you want to bolster your writing credentials, if you want to be taken more seriously as a writer, and if you want to set yourself apart from all the kids who claim to be published simply because they sent a poem to one of those Web sites that posts everything they receive—well, if you want any or all those things, it's time to move on. Start looking at bigger, more "adult" or mainstream markets aimed at a general readership, such as the feature or entertainment or Op-Ed sections—the page of comment and opinion opposite the editorial page (OPposite EDitorial, thereby Op-Ed.) The Op-Ed page is where you'll see opinion pieces by leading politicians, academics, and intellectuals. Look seriously at glossy national magazines. Could you do a story like the ones in those magazines? You don't necessarily have to completely stop writing for the school or local papers or sending your poems to Web sites. You can continue all those while starting to approach bigger and better markets. Aim high. After all, those bigger markets are where you can begin to win wider recognition for your writing—and where you can begin to earn serious money. That's also where ideas—your ideas—become more important.

A few young writers are fortunate enough to have regular gigs with newspapers or magazines. These often grow out of part-time internships or jobs such as office assistant (at newspapers these jobs are sometimes called copyboy or copygirl). Often they're the result of family connections; it's a lot easier to get a part-time job at a magazine if your mom's company is one of the magazine's biggest advertisers. But the teenagers lucky enough to get beginning part-time writing jobs at magazines or newspapers, no matter how they get them, all have to be good writers to keep those jobs. Sometimes they're staff writers, working a set number of hours or doing a set number of assignments or projects each week or month. Most young contributors to big newspapers and magazines, however, are freelancers who are paid according to how much of their work is accepted and published. Sometimes they submit a finished story, and the editor will either reject it, agree to publish (and pay for) it as is, or suggest that the writer make certain changes to the story and then re-submit it. Rather than submit a finished story, however, most freelance writers of every age prefer to submit a query—a summary of the story idea, preferably in a one-page letter or a brief e-mail. If it is a "cold" query, that is, from a writer to a publication that has never before published that writer's work, the query should include, in no particular order: the story idea, why the story is right for that publication, an introduction to the writer, and why this particular writer should be the one to do that story. (See Kelly James-Enger's "Tips from a Pro" on query letters on page 74, and the examples we've included of real query letters and e-mails on pages 76–80.)

Let's say you set a goal of getting a story published in the main daily newspaper in your area, whether it is the *Dallas Morning News* or the *Cedar Rapids Gazette*. In the regular newspaper, not in any special kids' section. Scan the paper to see what kinds of stories run in different parts of the paper. Look for the kinds of stories that you'd like to write—and that you *can* write. If you're not a jock and you don't know anything about sports, you're not going to be writing many articles for the sports section. If you love music and movies, look at the entertainment section. The family, health and lifestyle sections are also areas of newspapers that are typically more kid-friendly than, say, the general news sections. Similarly, if you want to break into a certain magazine, go online or to the library and read back issues to see if the magazine runs the type of story you want to do, and where it would best appear in the magazine. Remember that few big magazines are willing to take a chance on a writer they don't know—someone whose work they haven't published before—for a big feature story. To break in, to get a story published in a magazine for the first time, it's advisable to look for sections or departments that run smaller stories. Many magazines, for example, run little items, two hundred or three hundred words, in a section of briefs. Those smaller stories are a great place to start, and the editors of those sections always seem to be looking for sparkling little jewels from anyone and everyone who will offer them.

Once you've identified your target market, whether it's the entertainment section of your local paper or a department in a glossy magazine, do some additional market research. Does that section take material submitted by freelancers? Who's the editor? Does that editor prefer to receive submissions by e-mail, fax, or hard copies sent by snail mail? How much does the publication pay for the kind of articles you'd like to do? If you submit a story or a story idea, how long does it take for the editor to get back to you with a yes, no, or maybe? Some publications, especially magazines, have writer's guidelines on their Web sites that answer most of a potential freelancer's questions. Some magazines prefer to mail out guidelines and sample copies, and may ask you to pay for the sample copies. On the other hand, many publications, especially smaller magazines and most newspapers, do not publish submission guidelines. In that case, you call or e-mail and begin asking, "What's the procedure for submitting a story idea for such-and-such a section?" Some publications welcome unsolicited items and make it easy to submit them, while others don't take much content from freelancers and actively discourage submissions. No matter how perfect your story ideas are for a certain publication, nothing you say or do is going to convince editors who discourage submissions from freelancers that they should change their policy just for you.

Ah yes, story ideas. No matter how good a writer you are, no matter how much you like a publication, and no matter how much you want to be published there, it all comes back to ideas. As we said in our discussion about story ideas (chapter 3), the key to moving up to bigger and better markets is matching the right story to the right publication. The most common complaint magazine editors have about freelancers is, "It seems like they don't read the magazine. So many freelancers send us ideas for stories that are simply inappropriate for us. Or else they send us ideas for stories that we ran the month (or the day, or the year) before." Editors think it's a waste of time, both theirs and a writer's, for them to receive story ideas that they cannot use. They are looking for freelancers who will submit ideas that make them—the editors—look good. If you submit a story idea that an editor likes and assigns to you, and then you do a good job researching and writing the story, readers are going to like it. The editor will look good to his or her bosses. And that editor will look more kindly on your future story ideas, and begin to think of you when he or she has an assignment and is searching for a writer to take it on.

Let's look at some markets that we think are especially good for teenagers who are trying to kickstart their writing careers. Newspapers first. Most newspapers do not rely on freelance submissions for straight news, but do accept them in certain parts of the paper. Arts and entertainment, for example, or health and lifestyle, and other feature sections, sometimes accept work from freelancers. One of the best areas for freelancers in almost any newspaper, including big ones, is the travel section, especially in Sunday papers. Travel editors love stories that have a specific slant, including one with a youth slant. You can do this sort of story almost anywhere you go. In fact, we think the family vacation, or the weekend away, is always an opportunity for a travel story. One caution: don't try to do too much. If you spend a weekend in New York, don't pitch—or try to write—a story that encompasses everything about the Big Apple. Instead, pick something narrow and manageable. Maybe you come up with the idea for a story on "What Teenage Tourists Can Do in New York on a Summer Weekend," and then go through what you did, what was good or bad about it, and what else you might have done or might do next time. If you go to Bermuda, don't write everything about Bermuda. Maybe write about what it's like to spend an afternoon zipping around on those little rented scooters. If you go to Rome, don't try to describe every museum and cathedral. That's boring. Maybe write about how you spent three days trying to find the best gelato or Italian ice in the city.

Another one of the best markets for young writers is not so obvious. It's the Op-Ed page of the newspaper, traditionally one of the most "serious" pages. It's also a good market for young writers who have something to say. You're not going to get published very often on the Op-Ed pages, but it's a terrific clip and looks great on a resume. Look for your spots. What can you as a teenager contribute to the public debate and public knowledge over an issue? Earlier we mentioned Lizzie's first Op-Ed piece, in the Bergen County (N.J.) *Record,* when she complained about how security concerns in the months after September 11, 2001, were keeping many schools, including hers, from conducting the usual field trips. Why did the newspaper run that column? Well, everybody was and is concerned about national security. And almost everybody is concerned about local public education. In addition, the editors no doubt liked the fact that the piece was written by a teenager, from a student's perspective. There are always parents, teachers, administrators, school board members, consultants, professors, and various experts lining up to talk about what is best for kids. In Lizzie's column, here for a change was a *kid* talking about what's best for kids. Finally, Lizzie's column put forth a good argument: it didn't seem to make sense for schools to limit field trips for security reasons.

Fashion, entertainment, travel, Op-Ed—these are just a few of the sections that you might target as markets within your local newspaper. No doubt there are other sections that might accept freelance contributions from teenagers. But don't waste a lot of time working on stories before you know you have a place for them to get published. Make sure you know that your Sunday newspaper might actually buy your travel story before you spend a lot of time researching and writing it. It's difficult sometimes to pick up the phone and call an adult, a complete stranger, and ask questions: "Would you like a story from me about racing go-karts in Daytona? How many words would you like it to be? If you decide to publish it, how much will you pay me? Do you want to see my photos of the go-karts? Will you pay me for those, too?" But sometimes—many times—it has to be done. You have to make that phone call (a) to make sure you're not wasting your time, and (b) to get a foot in the door so that the editor knows who you are and what you are sending. Sometimes when a story arrives unsolicited, or even a proper query, an editor will barely look at it and toss it out. That's less likely to happen if the editor remembers, "Oh yeah, this is the kid who called me. That kid had spunk." Editors like spunk. So whether you're writing or speaking to an editor, be upbeat and positive. But not gushy—editors hate exclamation points and sucking up even more than they like spunk. If the editor says no, say, "Okay, thanks. Is it all right if I try you with another idea in the future?" If your hometown paper keeps rejecting you, try another one in the area. For example, if you're turned down by the *Chicago Tribune,* try the *Chicago Sun-Times.* If they say no, move on to the *Milwaukee Journal-Sentinel,* and so on. Once in a while, if a young freelance writer plays his or her cards right—and does a great job with story after story—the result can be one of those regular or semi-regular gigs at a newspaper. Say you've written several stories for your local paper's arts section about garage bands and up-and-coming young singer-songwriters in your town. The paper's arts editor knows you and trusts you. It might be worth a shot to go to the editor and say, "Hey, I notice you don't have anyone reviewing the latest music from famous groups, or writing about any of the big concerts in your area. How about if I do some reviews of new releases, and start reviewing concerts?" You never know. A few good stories might be all that's between you and a backstage pass when your favorite bands come through town.

The process of breaking into a new market is a little different when you're trying to get published in magazines. The bigger and better the magazine, as a rule, the more formal the process—and, naturally, the more difficult it is to get published. The bigger and better the magazine, the more likely its editors are to be looking for a formal query letter. And that query has to be sharp. (See the samples of Tim's query letters that follow this chapter.) The query letter not only introduces you and your idea, but also gives editors a first glimpse of you and your writing. If it's unprofessional in any way, your query is history. Many editors say they rarely read beyond the first sentence or two of a query. As soon as they lose interest—or, some say, as soon as they see an error of punctuation, spelling or grammar—they toss it. If a query is intriguing enough and professional enough to get them to read to the end, there's a good chance they're going to get in touch with the writer to talk about the idea. Ideas for magazines, by the way, typically must be more pointed, more focused, more unique, and more nuanced than ideas for newspapers. Again, it's supply and demand. Magazines don't require the sheer amount of writing that newspapers do, and since they cost more than newspapers their readers expect better, more informative, more entertaining reading. That's also why magazines usually pay more than newspapers—but we'll talk about money later in this chapter.

When you're aiming higher, you don't need to aim for the very top. There are often steps in between. Perhaps you'd love to write for *Teen Vogue* or *Sports Illustrated*. But maybe you're not ready for them yet. Or they're not ready for you. Maybe you can aim first to get a story into the fashion/lifestyle monthly for your area, or for one of the smaller magazine that focuses on a specific sport. Cast a wide net. Poke around at newsstands and in the doctor's office. Look at those free magazines that come in the mail. Look at specialty magazine and trade magazines. They've got stories in them, and somebody must write them. Why not you?

When you're doing your market research on a magazine, you're probably not going to need to pick up the phone and call an editor the way you would at your hometown newspaper. As we say, the process for pitching stories to magazines is more formal, and besides, magazine editors typically don't want to field calls from would-be writers they don't know. Many magazines have their writer's guidelines on their Web sites, but another good source to check is *Writer's Market,* the fat book that comes out annually with lists of hundreds of different magazines and details about their editors, what kind of stories they want, how much they pay, and so on. *Writer's Market* is a good present for a young writer, but if you don't want to ask for a book for your birthday or the holidays, it's at most public libraries. Besides going to it to check out magazines you know about, *Writer's Market* can also be invaluable for identifying targets you didn't even know existed. Suppose your family took an extended auto or RV vacation over the summer. Go to *Writer's Market* and look up the magazines for that region, travel magazines devoted to road trips, specialty magazines aimed at RV owners, and so on. Thumbing through *Writer's Market*, you'll be amazed at how many magazines there are, how esoteric some of them are, and how just reading about magazines you never heard of can give you an idea of a story you could write for them.

Let's pause and summarize here. There are different types of writing you can do: fiction, nonfiction, journals, satire, newspapers, magazines, books, and so on. There is an infinite range of subjects you can write about. There are innumerable ways you can research, organize, and write any given project, in many different styles or voices. And there are many different markets that might want to publish your writing.

The key to getting published is to find the right combination of the above. The right genre, the right idea, the right style, the right structure, and the right market. If any one of those isn't correct, what you've written probably won't get published. So consider all those factors in combination, working together, throughout the entire process. Don't pursue an idea without some confidence that you can do a competent, complete job on the research and reporting, and that you have a viable market for the finished product. Don't offer a story about cats to a magazine for dog owners. Don't send a sad story to a publication that is determinedly upbeat. Giving publications the kind of writing that they want and need is the best way to get published.

TIPS FROM A PRO:
Kelly James-Enger

First, look for a market you're familiar with. You're far more likely to write for a publication that you know than one you've never read before. Considering what types of stories and topics the magazine covers, start making a list of possible subject ideas that might fit there.

That's good advice for young writers from Chicago writer and coach Kelly James-Enger, whose freelance work has appeared in more than fifty national magazines, including *Redbook, Continental, Health, Woman's Day,* and *Self.* She's also the author of books including *Ready, Aim, Specialize! Create Your own Writing Specialty and Make More Money* (The Writer Books, 2003) and *The Six-Figure Freelancer* (Random House, 2005) and the novels, *Did You Get the Vibe?* (Strapless, 2003) and *White Bikini Panties* (Strapless, 2004). You can visit her Web site at www.kellyjamesenger.com.

James-Enger suggests that when you pitch a story idea, think about where it would belong in the magazine, and mention that in your query letter. Query letters, she says, should include four basic parts:

- a lead that catches the editor's attention;
- a paragraph that fleshes out the idea and convinces the

editor that his or her readers will be interested in the topic;

- a "nuts and bolts" paragraph that tells the editor more about the story, like who you plan to interview for the piece, how long it will be, and what section of the magazine it would be appropriate for (this lets the editor know you're familiar with his or her publication); and
- a paragraph that explains who you are, your writing experience, and any unique connection you have with the piece—like if you're proposing an article about someone who lives in your hometown.

One of the best ways to break into magazines, she says, is by pitching a short piece. If you haven't written for national magazines before, the editor may be a bit wary. He or she may not want to risk a full-length feature on a young writer who's an unknown quantity. Pitching shorter pieces for the front-of-the-book section of the magazine is a great way to get your foot in the door, gain experience, and prove yourself for longer assignments.

Of course, James-Enger says, when you contact an editor, you want to do your best work. Make sure you double-check your spelling and punctuation. Print out your query and read it out loud before you submit it—you'll catch more errors that way.

If an editor is interested, he or she will probably call and want to talk to you more about the idea. You want to make sure you know what your editor wants in terms of story length, sources, and angle so that you can deliver what he or she wants.

Also, make sure you confirm the deadline and how much the editor is willing to pay for the piece. Some smaller magazines and newspapers may not pay much, but your words are worth money—you should be paid for them.

James-Enger offers a final recommendation: don't give up if your first query or two doesn't sell. It often takes time and effort to break into national magazines. When you get a rejection, follow up immediately with a new query. Start off saying, "Thank you for your response to my query about (fill-in-the-blank). While I'm sorry you can't use it at this time, I have another idea for you to consider." Then include your new query. By doing this, you'll prove that you're persistent and professional—and you'll eventually nail an assignment.

SAMPLE PITCHES

Writers are always interested in seeing queries, especially those that resulted in assignments from good magazines. So we decided to include a brief sampling of Tim's pitches. First, here's a formal query that he sent to *The Atlantic Monthly* that resulted in an award-winning story, "Shoot to Kill." (You can read the full story on Tim's Web site, www.timharper.com). Note in the query that Tim tells a mini-story, while at the same time making it clear that he has a good main character who will help tell the story, and that he will also address larger issues, including what is going on elsewhere in the country and what experts are saying, pro and con, about this change in police tactics.

Dear Mr. Curtis:

I was in Peoria, Illinois, last weekend on some family business and went for a beer with one of my oldest friends, a longtime police officer. He told me that he and his fellow cops are going through new emergency-response training aimed at Columbine-like events. My buddy and the other cops are rattled because the new training is so different—opposite, he said—from what they were taught before. In the past, if one or more gunmen ran amok in a school or other building, the first officers at the scene were to secure the perimeters and wait for help. When more police arrived (often a SWAT team), they would start going in, carefully, securing parts of the building as they went. If there were injured people, getting them out and to a hospital was a priority. The goal was to pin down the gunmen, cut off escape routes, and then negotiate. The police were not supposed to shoot except when there was an immediate threat— shots being fired at them or bystanders.

The new training, according to my friend, requires the first officers at the scene to move in immediately, without securing the area. They are not supposed to stop to help wounded. If they see a gunman, the police are to shoot, and keep shooting. If a gunman is holding a gun to a kid's head, the police should shoot, and keep shooting. They don't want a gunman to hole up in a defensible position. The cops are supposed to attack and pursue, and keep the gunman moving if they can.

An abandoned office building in Peoria is being used for drills. Instead of those old cardboard pop-out figures, real people play the bad guys, with those new pepper-powder bullets. My friend had nasty welts where he'd been hit. He believes police departments around the country are being retrained this way. If you like, I can find out more about where, how and why this is happening. My friend says lawsuits and press criticism after Columbine are a big factor. I have to wonder, though, if this approach is really safer. I wonder what various experts have to say. Would this have saved lives at Columbine? Why wasn't this approach used before? What do cops themselves think of it? My friend wasn't sure, but he seemed uneasy.

Please let me know if you're interested, and what else you'd need to know before deciding if this is a possible story.

Sincerely,

Tim Harper

Next, let's look at a couple of quick ideas that Tim pitched to *Sky*, Delta's in-flight magazine, to an editor for whom he has done many stories and with whom he is personally friendly. Because they've worked together so long and know each other so well, Tim was able to adopt a much less formal tone.

Duncan,

A couple ideas, which I can develop more fully if you're interested . . .

- *Teaching kids ethics and morals at the computer. They spend almost as much time in front of computers today as they do in front of the TV. But some of what they're learning may not be good, beyond the usual concerns about violent games. It's okay to steal music, for example. It's okay to share homework or even test answers. It's okay to cut and paste other's work into papers. It's okay to trash friends in emails and IMs. It's okay to assume other identities and trash people, so that the person whose identity was "stolen" is blamed.*

- *The 100th anniversary of the first flight at Kitty Hawk is coming up in December. I'd love to do a piece about the Wright Brothers then and the commemorations now, including some stuff on the national monument at Kill Devil Hill, North Carolina. (Kitty Hawk was the closest town back then, but all that's there now is a plaque near the post office where reporters telegraphed out the first stories.) The stuff about the brothers is most interesting.*

Let me know if you want me to pursue either.
Cheers,
Tim

Incidentally, the first idea, the one about ethics online, resulted in a well-received story that spurred considerable reader reaction (you can read that one, too, on Tim's Web site). The strength of that story, even in such a brief pitch, was apparent: it provided useful information and perhaps challenged the thinking of many *Sky* readers—frequent fliers who were themselves parents and perhaps didn't pay enough attention to what their kids were doing online. The editor was not interested, however, in the second story idea, the one about the anniversary of the Wright Brothers' first flight. He said the magazine already had received many queries from other writers who wanted to do a similar story, and since it was going to get so much coverage in newspapers and on TV, rather than hire a freelancer like Tim to do a big story, *Sky* would probably do merely a brief piece written by a staff member.

A SAMPLE OP-ED:
"Give Us Our Field Trips"

GIVE US OUR FIELD TRIPS
By Elizabeth Harper
Bergen County (N.J.) Record, *April 2003*

For the past week and a half, my family and I have been hosts to a German exchange student named Katherina Troche. She's a pleasant, friendly girl and we've enjoyed having her stay in our home in Ridgewood. She also seems to enjoy attending classes with me at Ridgewood High School and seeing the sights in New Jersey and New York.

I've talked to Katherina a little bit about the differences she's noticed between life in Germany and life in America, and one thing in particular strikes me: while Ridgewood High School has not sent exchange students to any foreign country in the last two years, for the German group there was, Katherina said, "no question" of whether or not they would come to Ridgewood.

"I wasn't afraid," she said, "because the idea I could see America in this situation for a student-exchange was so exciting . . . None of the other students said they wouldn't travel to America."

This willingness to travel is a huge contrast from the Ridgewood school district's current policy prohibiting field trips out of Bergen County. This policy was handed down on February 14, more than a month before the war in Iraq began, and it remains in effect "indefinitely," according to a memo from Superintendent John Porter.

Besides the overseas exchanges, many other trips have been canceled. My history class was not allowed to make the half-hour bus ride to the Newark Museum. An overnight band trip to Philadelphia, rescheduled from last year, was canceled again this year. The school film club, of which I am a member, can no longer have official outings to see movies in New York.

Of course there have been heightened security concerns since September 11, 2001, and perhaps those concerns are greater since the war began. But it seems like my school, and others in Bergen County with similar restrictions, might be overreacting in declaring it too dangerous for students to travel across the ocean, the river, or even the county line. (It's not only our schools. A friend who lives in Manhattan goes back and forth to her high school in Brooklyn by subway every day, but her school prohibits field trips to Manhattan.)

In this month's *Outside* magazine, Daniel Glick wrote, "As Americans, it is not only our privilege but increasingly our duty to expand our horizons, to understand more about the world." He's right: we are holding ourselves captive by prohibiting school-led expeditions to New York or any other city.

Instead of isolating ourselves—as Bergen County residents and as Americans—shouldn't we be reaching out to connect with other people? As Glick put it, "Break down the barriers of fear through the warmth of human contact." Now is the time for sharing our culture and learning about other people's lifestyles. When we insulate ourselves from other nations, we increase the chances of misunderstanding each other.

There are many factors affecting whether or not Ridgewood students will be allowed to travel next year. Ms. Ruth Parks, my French teacher and the coordinator of this year's European exchange program, said, "We'll be doing an exchange as soon as we get permission from the Board of Education. As far as I'm concerned, I would have had a trip this year if not for the political situation. Next year it's our turn to go to Germany, but everything depends on the political situation."

My friend Whitney Clark, an RHS junior who is hosting Sylvia Korfmacher, another German student, says being a host has made her want to go on an exchange. "I feel that this whole experience has been really great," she told me. "It's made me want to take German next year and hopefully visit there on an exchange."

What I'm most afraid of is that from now on, the political situation will be seen as "too dangerous" for travel. When will the fear of terrorism end? When the war ends? When we catch Osama bin Laden? When every other country in the world declares their love for Americans? And if these things don't happen, will a whole generation of Americans grow up afraid to leave the country?

It seems like everyone is trying to get back to normal life, despite the war and a continued threat of terrorism. I don't think anyone should be forced to explore other countries and cultures. Parents and families can weigh the risks and decide for themselves whether it's safe for students to visit anywhere from the Newark Museum to New York to Germany. But students who want to travel deserve the option.

I don't want to see the exchange programs at my school or any other school slowly disappear because school administrators and board members think the rest of the world is too scary for us to visit. We should still have field trips and we should still have foreign exchanges. Let's not allow fear to become a normal part of life.

TIPS FROM A PRO:
Peter Grad

Do big daily newspapers like to get submissions from young writers? What do they look for? Peter Grad, the Op-Ed page editor at *The Record*, which serves Bergen County and other parts of northern New Jersey in the New York suburbs, seemed like a good person to ask—especially since he published two pieces by Lizzie while she was still in high school. Here's what he said in an e-mail:

We certainly welcome input from our younger readers. What we look for in submissions are the following:

- **Brevity:** It's important to make your point succinctly. Choose your words carefully. Articles should not exceed 750 words; often, a good opinion piece can be as short as 350 words. The best opinion pieces are crisp, tight, and pointed.

- **Clarity:** Get to the point, and do it clearly. Don't dance around the subject or present long, meandering anecdotes. Make it clear to the reader what your point is up-front.

- **Accuracy:** Do all necessary research to support your argument. Use reliable sources (newspapers, magazines, books, people), and feel free to quote experts or others knowledgeable about the subject you are tackling. Check for factual errors, grammatical errors, typos, and spelling errors.

- **Timeliness:** Speed is of the essence; choose a subject that is current, tackle it immediately, get it to us as soon as you can. Check to see if the subject has already been covered in the paper; editors don't like publishing stories covering the same areas as previous articles, unless there is a distinctive, new angle.

- **Artwork:** If you have a photo or drawing that helps illustrate your piece, inquire if the paper you are writing for accepts such artwork. Although the odds are not always high that we will publish accompanying art, it never hurts to send it along to us; we do print freelancers' artwork on occasion.

- **Confidence:** It is not a question of will your work ever be rejected; it often will be. We all have our work rejected at some time. Get used to it and get over it. Thank the editor of a paper who turns you down and start thinking of the next subject you want to write about. Keep your mind on your goal—to get published—and don't ever be discouraged.

Also, be sure to attach your name, address, and phone number on all correspondence. Include a biographical note about yourself, one or two sentences, with each submission (don't assume the editor will remember your bio).

One last tip, get familiar with the publication you are writing for. If you want to get published in *The Record,* for instance, be sure to read the Op-Ed and Editorial pages frequently to get a flavor of the kinds of articles that are written.

.7.

TIMING:
When to Write
for Whom

I N WRITING and getting published, as in so many aspects of
life, timing can be everything.

Over dinner one evening in March when Lizzie was a senior
in high school, we were all talking about what we were working
on and Lizzie happened to mention an assignment in her Advanced Placement English class. The class was studying Shakespeare, and everyone was supposed to write a takeoff on
Hamlet's soliloquy. You know, "To be or not to be, that is the
question . . ." We said it sounded like it could be a fun assignment, but Lizzie pointed out that the teacher, who runs the
class more like a college course and who acts more like a col-

lege professor than a high school teacher, could be very demanding. Plus he really liked Shakespeare. She'd have to put a lot of thought, and a lot of work, into the assignment to get a decent grade.

Her first problem: how to adapt the passage. One of her friends in the class was doing, "To Pee or Not to Pee," casting himself as a theatergoer who was agonizing over whether to get up and go to the restroom during a play—and thereby relieve his discomfort but call attention to himself and perhaps disrupt the play—or whether to sit tight and wait to make a dash at the final curtain. We started talking about ideas, and kept batting them around as we cleaned up after dinner. (See brainstorming, in the chapter on ideas.) Lizzie finally settled on a theme: To Beach or Not to Beach. Instead of the teenaged Prince of Denmark, her soliloquy would be spoken by a New Jersey teenager in the spring of his—or her—senior year, debating whether to join the rest of the class for a senior skip day and go to the Jersey Shore, or whether to listen to parents and teachers and stay back in school. She worked on it sporadically over the next few days, and didn't finish it—as usual—until the night before it was due. Tim asked if he could read it. (You can read it at the end of this chapter.)

"Hey, this is really good," Tim said. "It's too good to just turn it in for English class. Have you thought of submitting it somewhere?"

"Thanks," Lizzie replied. "Yeah, I thought it might be good enough to get published somewhere, but I don't know where."

"What about *The New Yorker*?" Tim suggested.

Her eyes grew wide. She was pleased and flattered. *The New*

Yorker, besides being at the top of the literary and journalism heap in America, is probably Lizzie's favorite magazine. When it arrives—usually on Mondays at our house—she makes a point of getting to the mail first and snaring it. Then the magazine often disappears into her room, or one of her book-and-magazine hidey-holes around the house, and the rest of the family has to ask for it or go looking for it.

"Do you think it's good enough?" she asked.

Tim shrugged. "Who knows? They run a lot of quirky stuff, and they like seasonal writing. There's only one way to find out. Send it in. The worst that can happen is they say no. Actually, the worst that can happen is no response at all. If they reject it, or if you haven't heard anything in two or three weeks, you can submit it somewhere else. Work your way down the food chain."

So Lizzie went online to *The New Yorker* Web site, looked up the submission guidelines and sent off her satirical soliloquy, "To Beach or Not to Beach," to the poetry editor of the magazine. Over the next month, Tim periodically asked if she had heard anything. The answer was always the same: not a peep.

"Well, when you don't hear anything, that's usually your answer," Tim said. "If you want, you can try to e-mail or phone the editor to make sure the piece was received." Lizzie said no, that if *The New Yorker* wanted "To Beach or Not to Beach," she probably would have heard something in a few days. She figured her rejection note, if one was coming at all, was waiting at the bottom of a stack of form rejection notes to be printed and mailed by an intern.

So she and Tim talked about where else to send the satirical soliloquy. He mentioned *USA Today,* which had published a number of his Op-Ed pieces in previous the years. Lizzie mentioned the Bergen County (N.J.) Record, our regional daily in northern New Jersey, which had published a couple of her Op-Ed pieces in previous months.

"Let's try *USA Today* first," Tim said. "You haven't been published there yet, I think they pay more for Op-Ed pieces than the *Record* does, and they usually let writers know pretty quickly whether they want an article or not. If they don't want it, you can still try the *Record.* We're still early enough in the spring season, but if you don't get it published by the time school is out in June, it's probably dead." Well, *USA Today* replied promptly, all right. They said no. A few days later, the friendly editor at the *Record* said no, too. He liked "To Beach or Not to Beach," himself, but thought it was a little "light" for the Op-Ed page.

At that point, we thought that was the end of "To Beach or Not to Beach." But before we tell you what eventually happened, it probably makes sense to look at where Lizzie sent that piece, and why. Where could or should she have sent it? It's a humor piece, so a logical choice might have been *MAD* magazine. But *MAD* usually prefers more low-brow humor. It's a piece that would have a lot of appeal to other high school seniors, perhaps, so maybe *Seventeen* magazine could be a market. But Lizzie had never seen anything quite like "To Beach or Not to Beach" in *Seventeen,* and it seemed like it would look out of place there. Moreover, glossies such as *Seventeen* typically have a three-to-six-month lead time between when they receive submissions and when they run them. The graduating-senior, Skip Day appeal of "To Beach or Not to Beach" would have been wasted on *Seventeen* because the magazine couldn't run the piece until springtime had passed. (Although many magazines are willing to hold good seasonal pieces til the next year.) That's why timing is so important when proposing seasonal stories. You need to consider when a publication will be looking for those stories. If you want to write a story about someone who has invented a new type of snow shovel, for example, you don't want to propose it in winter, when a publication is considering summer stories. And you don't want to propose a story about someone who designs summery swimwear when a publication is looking for winter stories. Most publications are happy to tell writers when they are looking for seasonal stories, but it's pretty much a matter of common sense, especially for food, fashion, leisure, lifestyle, and travel publications.

Since "To Beach or Not to Beach" was timely, or seasonal, and had an expiration date—graduation day—it needed to be offered to publications that could get it into print quickly. That's why Lizzie tried daily newspapers, which typically have a lead time for features of a week and sometimes only a day or two, and *The New Yorker*, a weekly that has a lead time of only a few weeks. And that's why we all but gave up hope of seeing it in print after it wasn't snapped up by *The New Yorker* or *USA Today* or the *Record*. It was only a couple of weeks til graduation, and she hadn't found a place to publish the piece. It was almost out of date.

But then one of those wonderful coincidences came along,

one of those little nuggets of luck that sometimes fall out of nowhere and clunk unsuspecting writers on the head. A friend sent Tim an e-mail saying that she knew an editor who was temporarily in charge of arts and entertainment coverage for the New Jersey section of the Sunday edition of *The New York Times* and was looking for story ideas. We sent "To Beach or Not to Beach," to the *Times* editor out of the blue. The editor replied promptly, saying no, sorry, this wasn't something he could use as an arts or entertainment story. But he did like the piece. He said he had forwarded "To Beach or Not to Beach" to another editor who might be able to use it. A few days later, the second editor sent a note saying yes, he liked "To Beach or Not to Beach," and a few days after that Lizzie had her first byline in the *New York Times*. Timing was everything. Well, maybe not quite everything. Certainly it was good timing to offer a satirical piece about senior skip day during the early spring. But persistence was important, too. "To Beach or Not to Beach" never would have been published if it hadn't been offered to five different editors—one at *The New Yorker,* one at *USA Today,* one at the *Record,* and two at the *New York Times.* And finally, maybe there was a bit of luck involved, in that an editor at the *Times* let it be known there was a need for stories for the New Jersey section. But it helped that Lizzie's timing put her in a position to be lucky.

SAMPLE FEATURE:
"To Beach or Not to Beach"

TO BEACH OR NOT TO BEACH
By Elizabeth Harper
The New York Times, *June 2004*

Note: At this time of year, despite warnings and threats from teachers and parents, it is traditional for high school seniors in northern New Jersey to have a spontaneous "senior cut day," and skip school to pile into cars and head down the Garden State Parkway to spend the day on the Jersey Shore, sunning and splashing. In this recasting of Shakespeare, one student imagines Hamlet not as the Prince of Denmark but as a high school senior torn between what she's supposed to do and what she wants to do.

> *To beach, or not to beach—that is the question:*
> *Whether 'tis nobler in the mind to suffer*
> *The slings and arrows of outrageously long school days*
> *Or to take cars to the sea and sunshine*
> *And by going have fun. To lie, to sunbathe*
> *Once more, and by sunbathe to say we end*
> *The paleness, and the thousand natural shocks*
> *That flesh is heir to. 'Tis a consummation*
> *Devoutly to be wished. To lie, to sunbathe,*
> *To sunbathe—perchance to tan—ay, there's the rub,*

For in that bronze of skin what wrinkles may come
When we have shuffled past this youthful vanity
Must give us pause. There's the skin cancer
That makes calamity of so long tanning.
For who would bear the whips and scorns of school,
Th' oppressor's essays, the impossible tests,
The pangs of despised pop quizzes, the bell's delay,
The insolence of the attendance office, and the spurns
That patient merit of th' unworthy takes,
When she herself might the Parkway take
To the beach? Who would fardels bear,
To sit and daydream under an indoor life,
But that the dread of UV rays in the sun,
The outdoor country, from whose bourn
No traveler returns unsunburned, puzzles the will,
And makes us rather bear that skin tone we have
Than tan to others that we know not of?
Thus conscience does make cowards of us all,
And thus the native hue of my skin
Stays sicklied o'er with the pale cast of thought,
And beach trips of great pitch and moment
With this regard their enthusiasm turns awry
And lose the name of fun.

Tamekia Reece

Before she was even ten years old, Tamekia Reece won a school writing competition and was published for the first time in a school district newsletter. A few years later, she was published again on a Web site she describes as "a scam." But this modest start didn't stop her from aiming higher. "At the time I thought it was great that I was going to be published," she remembered, "but later I realized they publish pretty much anything. But I felt I had talent, so I kept trying."

Her persistence paid off (literally) when a true-life story, "Without Him," was accepted by the *Chocolate for Teens* series. After just one rewrite, her acceptance letter was accompanied by a check for one hundred dollars. "Seeing that first check in my name made me feel great! I was published and paid!" she said.

Since that first success, Tamekia has been published—and paid—for her articles on teen life by magazines and Web sites including *Seventeen, Girls' Life,* Planned Parenthood, Black Enterprise, *Women's Health & Fitness,* and *Listen* Magazine. Mostly, she writes about teen dating issues like abstinence, cheating, and how to communicate with boyfriends/girlfriends. She also writes for parents on topics like teen lingo.

Tamekia, who lives in Houston and is now twenty-two, said that the only disadvantage she found as a teen writer was that "sometimes editors and other writers don't take you seriously." Once, when approached by an editor at a national magazine, she was afraid that her age would disqualify her for the assignment.

It turned out, though, that the editor thought she'd be perfect, as a young writer, to write the piece on teens. She also advises teens to be professional when dealing with adults, and not to post too much of their work on message boards. Don't risk losing your good ideas to older or better-connected writers. As Tamekia found, age discrimination will disappear "once you prove you've got the goods!"

JONNY: THE LITTLE BROTHER GETS INTO THE ACT

When Lizzie gets involved in something new, her younger brother Jonny often dabbles in it, too. When she started playing the flute in fifth grade, Jonny, then in second grade, took up the clarinet. And when Lizzie began getting published, both in her school paper and the *Ridgewood News,* Jonny decided to try writing.

His first publishing opportunity came at age thirteen, when he and Tim made a two-month cross-country trip in the Harper family station wagon. They reserved spots on the couches of friends and family members all across America, and then set out for a summer of adventure. Before leaving, Jonny offered to e-mail weekly updates on the duo's progress back to the *Ridgewood News.* The paper's editors liked the idea, so every Sunday he would haul out Tim's laptop, usually resting it on his lap while riding in the passenger seat of the Volvo, and chronicle the week's events.

He reported on roadside attractions (like Carhenge—

Stonehenge recreated with old cars in Nebraska), cultural stops (including the Rock and Roll Hall of Fame in Cleveland), and with special enthusiasm, fireworks. After checking out every fireworks warehouse in the Midwest, the Volvo was soon bristling with bottle rockets, Roman candles, and some big rockets that were just labeled "municipal display quality." As Tim observed, "If Volvo had equipped its vehicles like this in World War II, we'd all be speaking Swedish now."

People back at home in Ridgewood kept up on the trip by reading Jonny's articles. We didn't realize what a pyromaniac reputation he was getting until Nancy, taking a cab to the airport on the way to meet up with Tim and Jonny in Los Angeles, heard from her driver about some fireworks-loving kid who was traveling around the country with his dad and writing about it. "That's my son!" she told the surprised driver.

The following summer, when Jonny was fourteen, he resumed his unofficial post as the *Ridgewood News's* Cool Summer Activity Correspondent by writing an article about his experience at Outward Bound surfing camp in Costa Rica. This time, he even got paid, in a way—in return for the publicity generated by the article, Outward Bound knocked two hundred dollars off his tuition. Plus, all the people who had laughed at Jonny's explosive exploits the summer before were now admiring the accompanying photo of him, tanned and leaning against his surfboard with the Pacific Ocean in the background.

Jonny hasn't taken on any more writing assignments since then, but maybe he's just waiting for the right wave to come along. What subjects would bring him out of early retirement? "Something even cooler," he suggests, ". . . like skydiving."

. 8 .

RESEARCH AND WRITING:
How to Be Productive

YOU HAVE AN IDEA, and you have a market in mind where you'll try to get it published. What's left? Writing the story.

A common mistake is assuming that the writing is the most important part of the equation. It's not. Writing is necessary, of course, but the really critical thing is the story. It's what hooks readers from the beginning and keeps them interested in your work. Storytelling, one of the oldest art forms, is still an important writing skill. Without some human element that readers can relate to, your story will be dry and boring. Besides, if you don't know what story you're telling, you have nothing to write. Don't make the mistake of emphasizing your writing over the story.

Usually, an idea—even a great one—needs some extra thought and development to become a story. This is where research comes in. Research is sometimes as easy as talking to your parents or friends about their opinions and experiences. Other times you can do a quick Google search, say, if you want to write about scuba diving, and come up with a detailed history of diving and famous divers. If your subject is more specific, you might have to contact experts or people with special knowledge of the field. The best writing incorporates general background—facts you could find online or in an encyclopedia—with more specialized information you unearth through reporting.

Consider the different ways you could research an article on World War II, for example. First, there is the basic information: who fought, when, and why? That's common knowledge, available in textbooks and encyclopedias. Then there are the details, like exact dates, names of famous battle sites, and important wartime leaders. You can learn those from books or Web sites dedicated to World War II. Finally, there are firsthand sources: veterans and other people who were alive at the time. Maybe your grandparents can help, or residents of a local nursing home. You can also check town records to see who in your area fought in World War II. Using any or all of these methods will bring you closer to the goal: finding your story. What angle, what perspective will you bring to the issue?

For instance, staying with the World War II example, imagine that you interview a veteran and get the chance to look through his combat diary. You can incorporate his own first-person observations into the story of the war as a whole—for instance, his account of a buddy's death in a big battle alongside facts about where his company was and how many men survived.

The more research you do, the better you understand your subject. Just taking the time to read a few extra articles or talk to a few more people can unearth a few more interesting facts, and it's those little touches that will absorb readers. Even seemingly insignificant details—the color of your grandfather's hair, the fact that he wore a hat—will bring your subject to life.

Research is never totally complete—you can continue learning about your subject and adding to your piece right up until you submit it to an editor—but when you feel like you have a good base to begin writing, it's time to organize everything you want to say by writing down your ideas. There are dozens of strategies for doing this. Some people like using mind webs, where you start by writing down one central idea and then connect secondary points to the main one. The final result looks like a spider web, with lots of lines radiating out from your thesis. Another approach, one that works particularly well for narratives, is writing out your ideas, plot points, or events on index cards. Then you can physically arrange and rearrange them on a table, bulletin board, or other flat surface until you find the perfect sequence. This method is usually called a time line or story board.

Another way to organize your thoughts before writing is to make an outline. Some people love outlining, others hate it. But give it a try before you decide. It's up to you; your outline can be as simple or as detailed as you choose. Start by making headings of all your main ideas. For instance, the local elementary school is under construction because (a) its heating system is outdated, (b) there might be high levels of asbestos, and (c) the incoming classes are bigger than the school's capacity. Then, you can add more information in subheadings below each main point.

To Lizzie, outlining is a valuable planning tool, but she rarely does it the same way twice. Many of her *Ridgewood News* columns began as outlines that were really more like lists of questions: How does our clothing express who we are? or What effect will this new school policy have on students? Then she lists her answers and comments under the questions. That way, she has a way to introduce the subject, and instead of trying to mentally keep track of every idea, they're all arranged neatly on paper.

Sometimes she bypasses the question stage and just jots down ideas. At the dinner table, at school, wherever she gets a chance to brainstorm, Lizzie can begin the writing process with just a pen and a slip of paper. (She wasn't always this organized—it's taken a few years for her to realize that good ideas will disappear forever if you don't write them down.) Each of her quick ideas can then become a heading in a more developed outline, to be fleshed out with subheadings and details.

Both Lizzie and Tim use lists to get organized. Even before you start to write, you can use lists for research. What are all the books you want to take out from the library? Which questions do you want to remember to ask this interview subject? If you don't write them down, you risk forgetting them and losing what could have been a valuable piece of information.

When you have a clear idea of what you're going to write and how you're going to write it, start getting everything down on paper. One common misconception among young writers is that when you finally begin, you have to start at the beginning of a story or article. Not true. In fact, many writers like to do the end first so they know where they're going. Or you can start off by figuring out the middle pieces. Basically, there isn't just one way to begin writing. Your own strategy will depend on your subject, the kind of story you're writing, and the amount and quality of your research. Even if you don't think a certain sentence or paragraph really fits with your idea of the piece as a whole, leave it in until you've completed the whole thing. You never know—maybe if you switch a few things around, it'll work perfectly. It's always easier to go back and delete things or edit them down than to fill in holes where you should have written more.

Preparation is the key: If you've done a lot of research and made a comprehensive outline of your material, you'll find it's pretty easy to write. You might get stuck, but over time you'll develop tricks—every writer has them—to help yourself keep going. Tim, for instance, visualizes each chunk of information as a piece of furniture he's moving into a house. Just as you don't put all the furniture right inside the door of a new house, Tim doesn't pile up information at the beginning of a story. Instead, he thinks about the work as a whole and decides where everything belongs. It's like walking through a house, choosing where to hang a picture. Once your foundation is laid, you just have to build it up. This tactic works for pretty much every form, from short stories to magazine articles. For longer work, like books, it's the same thing—just with more research and material.

When you're writing, hold the reader's attention by keeping the story in motion. Don't let it get stagnant; use narrative to move the story along sequentially. Explain events and their causes—the local auto plant moved its operations overseas, for example, so many of your neighbors are out of work. In this situation, you might want to even focus on the story of one person who lost a job. The human angle is important because it often shows the furthest-reaching effects of a big story, like how a family is affected financially and emotionally when one parent is unemployed. If that's the point of your story, though, don't spend too much time explaining other aspects. While it might be tempting to digress, keep a tight focus on your intended subject. Tim always makes sure he can sum up the whole point of a story in one sentence. This sentence, which would be his reply if a friend asked him what he was writing about, is the core of the piece. Everything else, every single point, relates back to that central idea.

It's also important to be sure that your story's structure makes sense. Important and interesting things deserve attention, so don't bury them in a dense paragraph. You can use funny anecdotes, even short ones, to liven up the story and keep it moving along. If you're profiling your school's new science teacher, for example, a story about one of her early lab experiments (did she blow anything up?) could provide a funny twist. It might even be a good way to introduce her. ("Ms. Smith has come a long way since her days of wreaking havoc in her own high school chemistry lab to become a teacher in ours.")

No matter what style you're writing in—fiction or nonfiction, news article or short story—the beginning, or lead, is crucial. It needs to practically reach out and grab the reader so that he or she is interested enough to read the whole thing. The ideal lead gives some unusual, fascinating, or useful piece of information to pique the reader's curiosity; it could be a statistic, provocative quote, or anecdote that "leads" the reader into the story. If you start off with one person, either quoting him or telling his story, it's a good idea to get back to that person again at some point in the piece. Sometimes you can even use the resolution (or lack thereof) of his situation in the end of your story to neatly wrap the whole thing up.

When you get down to writing the actual meat of your story, don't worry about making it perfect in the first draft. Even the most organized writers make mistakes in the construction of their stories, and one of the most common offenses is the overuse of adjectives and adverbs. Your readers don't want to be told what a story means; instead, it's better to describe a situation or issue and let them decide for themselves what it's all about. This basic rule—*show, don't tell*—is a favorite of English teachers as well as editors. Why bother summarizing everything from your own point of view when you can just give the facts?

Tim once knew a Pulitzer Prize–winning journalist named Saul Pett who had interviewed Harry Truman. Pett managed to capture the former president's personality in just a few sentences, without unnecessary adjectives or adverbs, by simply describing how Truman sat in his office behind a huge, immaculate desk. On the desk was a pencil holder. Each of the pencils was sharpened to a perfect point, and each one's eraser was worn almost completely down. Without telling the reader directly that Truman was a fastidious man who worked meticulously, Pett still managed to get the impression across.

This example also shows the power of the anecdote. Whenever possible, you should substitute a quick, but illuminating, story like the one above in the place of worn adjectives. Anecdotes help readers get to know your subject in a way that ordinary descriptions cannot. Think about it: would you rather be told that a character is messy, or get a colorful description of her bedroom's disarray? Like the saying goes, a picture is worth a thousand words. Use words to paint an imaginary picture for your readers.

At the end of your piece, avoid summarizing or drawing conclusions. Let the reader decide. Little kids and immature writers often use trite expressions like "I hope you enjoyed my story about . . ." or "In conclusion, . . ." to wrap up a story they don't know how to end. Instead of falling into the summary trap, try using a funny, poignant, or, in some way, telling anecdote or quote. It'll leave a more lasting impression than a basic summary of everything you already said. Another good way to end a story is by looking ahead and presenting a forecast, most often with a quote or anecdote, of the issue's future.

As Robert Cormier, author of *The Chocolate War,* said, "The beautiful part of writing is that you don't have to get it right the first time, unlike, say, a brain surgeon." Your first draft is a good start, but you're not finished with the piece yet. Read through it carefully, several times, to make sure you haven't included any typos or spelling mistakes. Most computers have spell checking features, but don't rely on them to catch your mistakes. If you wrote "you're car," for instance, where you should have written "your car," a computer wouldn't catch the error because the word is technically spelled right, even though it's used incorrectly. It also helps to read your work aloud to hear how it flows; sometimes, awkward sentences look fine on the page but sound horrible aloud. Many writers forget this stage in the rush to finish a piece or meet a deadline, but it's a good technique for gauging the readability of your writing.

Errors in spelling, grammar, and punctuation aren't the only ways to inadvertently lower the quality of your writing. You can also weaken your work by incorrectly quoting sources or including factually inaccurate material. That's why, if you're conducting an interview, it's important to take careful, complete notes and tape-record, if necessary. Whether or not you tape-record an interview depends on convenience, length of the interview, your note-taking skills, and of course whether you own a tape recorder—but no matter what you decide, make sure the quotes are completely accurate. Double-check all of your facts, especially unsubstantiated information from interviews and other sources. There's no easier way to undermine your credibility with an editor than by submitting material containing incorrect information.

Before you can use any of this advice, of course, you have to write something. And the first step in writing is the first word. So if you're having trouble with writer's block and can't get started, here's some advice: just do it. You don't have to write the first word of the story first; you can write the last one first, if that's easier for you. No matter what creative difficulties you face, start by writing something that flows—the setting, maybe, or a description of your characters. Once you've gotten the creativity brewing with those exercises (whose results you may or may not use in the finished piece) you'll be in the mind-set to write the real thing.

Tim Says:
NEVER ASSUME

If you're doing journalism, or any sort of non-fiction, every word you write has to be true. You can't assume that it's true, or hope that it's true. Suppose I come into your English or journalism class. I open my brief-case, pull out a full Poland Spring bottle, open the top and take a healthy drink.

"What did you see?" I ask you and your classmates. "How would you describe what just happened if you were writing about it in a story?"

Most students would say, "You took a drink of Poland Spring water." Some students might add details: it was a one-pint bottle, for example, or it was a plastic bottle, or it was a bottle of Poland Spring *mineral* water. They're not necessarily correct. They're making assumptions. What if the bottle actually held tap water I put into it that morning? You might assume it was Poland Spring mineral water because it's in a Poland Spring bottle, but for all you know I could be belting down gin or vodka.

Any statistic, any fact, any assertion, or any claim needs to be attributed or sourced—unless you are willing to take the responsibility for it yourself. If someone you interview tells you that the quarterback is going to miss the next game with an injury or that the school board is going to cancel all field trips because of budget cuts, your story should either attribute the statement to the source—by name—or you should confirm the facts with someone else who would know for sure if the statement is true. A careful journalist would do both—attribute the statement, but at the first opportunity confirm with other sources. When you get primary sources disagreeing with what you've been told—the quarterback says he's not injured but is instead academically ineligible, or the school board says it is only canceling some field trips, not all—then you have a much more interesting story because someone, for whatever reason, is not telling the truth.

In my Poland Spring example above, the students should have asked me to confirm that I was drinking Poland Spring water.

Marty Beckerman

When he was little, Marty Beckerman loved to write and illustrate his own comic books, featuring original characters like Fluffy the Ninja Mouse and Hair Tonic Man. He'd photocopy the comics and staple them together before selling them at his elementary school—an early version of self-publishing.

Later, at age seventeen, Marty got into self-publishing again. This time it was a real book, called *Death to All Cheerleaders: One Adolescent Journalist's Cheerful Diatribe Against Teenage Plasticity.* This book happened as a result of his experiences as a humor columnist for the *Anchorage* (Alaska) *Daily News.* He'd been writing for the *Daily News'* Perfect World teen section since he was fifteen, chronicling teen life and issues such as school, activities, and dating—well, trying to get dates.

"When I started out, all I read was Dave Barry," Marty said. "I worshiped at the altar of Dave Barry. My goal in life was to be the young Dave Barry. Not that I stole his jokes, but I definitely borrowed his tone and writing voice. I was derivative, not very creative." As Marty got older, his influences expanded to include Hunter S. Thompson, Bret Easton Ellis, and Orson Scott Card. With more experience and a more "evolved" writing style, he branched out into "new subjects and new angles."

Based on the modest success of *Death to All Cheerleaders*, more writing opportunities started popping up for Marty. John Strausbaugh, then editor of the *New York Press*, loved the book.

After interviewing Marty for the *Press,* he offered him a column. Suddenly, at seventeen, Marty was writing for New York's second-largest weekly paper. Strausbaugh also introduced him to a literary agent, which led to a book deal with MTV/Pocket Books (an imprint of Simon & Schuster) for Marty's second book, *GENERATION S.L.U.T.* [sexually liberated urban teens]: *A Brutal Feel-Up Session With Today's Sex-Crazed Adolescent Populace.*

Marty, at twenty-one and recently graduated from American University, had some good advice for other aspiring young writers: read as much as you can. "If you only read one author," he said, "you'll sound like that author. Nobody wants another writer they've already read." He also recommended playing the "young writer" card to your advantage. "Being young can be a selling point . . . there are some things you can get away with, things you can say at sixteen or seventeen, that an older writer wouldn't." When you're not a teenager anymore, he realized, "now you're a twenty something writer and the league is so much bigger. . . . Writing is a competition in a lot of ways."

"Being a teen writer was my gig," he said, "but I can't pretend I still know what it's like to be a teenager anymore." Teens, living through high school, are in the best position to write in the classic "teen angst" genre. Plus, he said, "If I wrote about teen sex anymore the feds would get involved—*Generation S.L.U.T.,* especially, summed up my adolescence; it was my bittersweet kiss good-bye to not-so-innocent youth."

Now he's working on a book, called *Nation of Retards* "about how political and ideological forces try to get into the educational system and the media." He compares the book's style to those of Michael Moore and Bill O'Reilly, though his own views don't fit with theirs. Having gotten his start as a teen writer, "it's time for me to step up to the plate and be a real writer." But he'll remember the lessons he learned from being published so young, as well as its rewards—a few years ago, he even got to meet the man who inspired him to write in the first place: Dave Barry.

YOUR SPACE:

When and Where to Write

ONCE YOU KNOW WHY and what you want to write, there are the issues of when, where, and how you will do it. It's all up to you. Your own style and preferences determine the basis of your physical approach to writing.

The first step is setting up your office. Of course, very few teen writers have their own personal office, but it's important to think of your workstation—whether it's a desk in your bedroom or a corner of a parent's home office—as the headquarters of your own writing operation. It's the launching pad for your potentially great writing career.

For most teen writers, school is the equivalent of a full-time job. It's how they spend their days (and afternoons and evenings, doing homework). If school is work, writing should be pleasure—and you can often use the same materials for both. Your arrangement for keeping track of school assignments, completing them, and turning them in on time can double as a system for managing writing projects. Do you use a planner or homework assignment pad? Consider using another one for writing. Do you like a certain type of pen for writing school essays? Buy an extra box of them for jotting down notes. The tricks you've discovered that work well for you at school will be handy at home, too.

Every writer needs, at the bare minimum, a desk or flat surface, a good chair, and a word processor. Although typewriters are still used, they've been almost completely replaced by computers. Besides the obvious benefits of increased power and capability, including Internet access, using a computer is practically necessary because most publications want digital copies of submissions to avoid the task of retyping or scanning them. The family computer will work just fine, and if you're lucky enough to have your own computer, that's even better. You'll also learn to take advantage of family resources, such as envelopes, stamps, and paper.

If you're using the family telephone to do interviews or contact editors, try to make sure no one picks up the phone and interrupts you—though the Internet has made phone communication less vital than it once was. Most correspondence with editors can now be conducted via e-mail. It's easier and cheaper, too. We personally prefer e-mail because it's less formal and allows more time to compose a message, rather than feeling "on the spot" on the phone. If you do use the phone a lot, make sure to clear it with your parents—a giant phone bill is never a welcome surprise.

The key to setting up a workstation where you can be productive is recognizing your needs. Then you can fulfill them at the minimum amount of cost and angst with the maximum gain. If you can get multiple uses out of one piece of equipment, that's great. For instance, when you realize that your computer's monitor is too low, find a creative solution (such as placing an old textbook under it for added height). It's easy, it's cheap, and it'll help you avoid the time-consuming and painful headaches that come from an awkwardly positioned monitor.

There are other physical factors to consider when you're setting up your workstation. A good chair is the key to an ergonomic, or body-friendly, space. The chair may sound unimportant—just a place to rest your butt while you write, right?—but your chair can really affect your body and, in turn, your desire and ability to write. When you choose a chair, make sure its height allows you to rest your feet flat on the floor and your wrists naturally on the desk. It should also let you look straight at the computer's monitor, not up or down. Make sure that your chair provides adequate back support, too.

Ergonomics go beyond how you sit, of course. You have to also consider your routine movements, like reaching for printer paper or twisting over to the bookcase. Awkward stretches and maneuvers are harmless once or twice a day, but when you do the same thing over and over again, day after day, it can take a toll on your muscles and joints. It might sound silly—most teen writers are too young to be at risk for repetitive-stress injuries—

but creating good habits and working ergonomically now may help you avoid problems later, especially if you plan to pursue writing as a career.

After assuring the physical comfort of your office, it's time to nourish the spirit. A good way to do this is let as much natural light in as possible. Sunlight is healthier and more pleasant, generally, than harsh fluorescent light. When you're writing at night, use bulbs that come closest to natural light. If possible, a window with a view will improve your writing environment, too. One study even found that a window with a view of vegetation can improve workers' mental and memory function by 10 to 25 percent. If you don't have a great view, or even a flower box outside your window, you can hang up pictures from vacations or even magazines for inspiration. Whatever puts you in a creative, productive mood.

It can be really fun to set up your own "office," even if the arrangement is no fancier than a desk in your room. But keep the goal in mind: a comfortable place where you'll be inspired to write. Distraction and procrastination will be two of your greatest enemies. Even when you love writing and can't wait to finish a project, it's easy to get sidetracked with "busywork." Busywork is anything that puts off the task at hand. For Lizzie, it's checking e-mail and chatting online with friends. And cleaning up her desk. And doing laundry. And countless other useful, noncrucial undertakings.

When you write at home, there are always distractions. The key is to recognize them and manage their effect on your productivity. Set limits to how much busywork you'll do before getting down to real business; decide on fifteen minutes of surfing the Internet, for example, and then an hour of uninterrupted writing. If your writing space offers particularly irresistible distractions (the TV comes to mind), just unplug them, or get them out of there completely.

Without your own private workspace, however, there will always be intrusions you can't escape. For many teen writers living at home, the biggest disturbance is the rest of the family. Just when you're really buckling down and getting some work done, Mom will come in to say that it's time for dinner. Or your brother will want to use the computer for his homework. Whatever the issue is, you probably can't escape it. They're your family, after all, and you do live with them.

While you can't demand a totally distraction-free environment from your family, you can adopt certain strategies to keep relations smooth and avoid conflict while you're trying to write. First, explain to the other residents of your home (Mom, Dad, siblings, relatives, whoever) your writing goals and their potential benefits. You want an outlet for your mind's fantastic stories, or you think that colleges will be impressed by your collection of newspaper clips. Whatever your own reasons for writing, describe them so that your family understands exactly why it's so important to you.

Later, you should offer specifics about your writing needs. This includes time on the family computer, if necessary, and a quiet, peaceful place to think. Agree on where you'll keep all the stuff that a writer accumulates, such as clips, files, drafts, and supplies. You'll get more help and support from your family when they appreciate your attitude and approach to writing.

Before you share it with your family, though, you have to

develop the approach that works for you. This involves figuring out your own optimal writing conditions. They're different for everyone. When you write, is it in long, industrious stretches or short, intensely creative bursts? In the daytime or at night? After a meal or before? When you're excited or when you're relaxed? Listening to music or in complete silence? Does it bother you if other people are in the room? Can you focus on writing if you're hungry, for instance, or tired? Your answers to these questions and countless others determine your unique writing style. Some people are fussy about how they write; others can do it anywhere, in any conditions. We're closer to the anywhere-anytime variety of writers, with a few key differences: Tim is sometimes happiest writing when there's a baseball game on the radio, but Lizzie prefers listening to CDs. Find the place that works best for you: somewhere at home, at a library, bookstore, coffee shop, wherever. Maybe, as a teen writer, your most productive time is during a free period at school. It's up to you and your own powers of concentration.

Once you've figured out your best environment for writing, stick to it. If it works well for you, why change? Make it part of your routine to write in the style you're most comfortable with; that way, your passion won't become a chore. If you have the time between school, sports, and activities, set aside a short period every day to write. It doesn't have to be a huge commitment—you can get a lot done in less than an hour a day. Otherwise, dedicate a few hours every weekend to writing.

Even if you aren't writing on assignment for a magazine or newspaper, it's a good idea to set deadlines for yourself. Deadlines are a powerful motivational tool; they make you sit down and write even when you aren't really in the mood. You can make meeting your own deadlines worthwhile by rewarding yourself; for example, take a quick snack break after writing five hundred words of your short story. Then save the rest of the cookies for after you've finished the whole thing. This technique will serve you well in other areas of life, as well. Schoolwork obviously improves when you know how to manage deadlines, but the ability to motivate and discipline yourself can also help you succeed in sports, playing a musical instrument, and learning other skills.

It's also a good idea to develop a system for keeping track of your projects and deadlines. There are low-tech and digital options, ranging from a whiteboard or bulletin board on your wall to a computerized calendar you keep and regularly update. There's an added benefit to writing down goals and deadlines—when you've accomplished something, there's no feeling quite like crossing it off the list.

Every writer has his or her "dream office"—the place he or she would love to work if time, money, location, whatever allowed. Very few, if any, actually have that perfect place. Teen writers are subject to the same constraints as their adult counterparts, and often to an even greater degree because they live at home with their parents. But with some ingenuity (and your family's cooperation) you can make the humblest corner of your home a workspace that's pleasant, calm, and above all conducive to writing. You just need to recognize how, where, and when you write best—then create an environment where those needs are fulfilled.

TIPS FROM A PRO:
Sally Wendkos Olds

Even if you're not selling regularly or accumulating impressive stacks of assignments, you should be writing every day. This will enable you to improve your craft and get into the routine that most professional writers follow. They don't wait for inspiration; they write.

That's what one successful freelance writer, Long Island–based Sally Wendkos Olds, tells would-be writers, and she follows her own advice by writing as much as possible. Within her specialties of child development, family life, relationships, health, and travel, she has published more than two hundred articles and authored or coauthored ten books. Her work has appeared in magazines such as *McCall's, Woman's Day, Redbook, Ladies' Home Journal, Working Woman, Mademoiselle, Ms., New York Times Magazine, Newsday Magazine,* and *Reader's Digest,* as well as *The New York Times* and other major newspapers. Her most recent book, *A Balcony in Nepal: Glimpses of a Himalayan Village* (iUniverse, 2002), combined two of her favorite subjects, travel and human relationships, in an account of her experience as one of the first Western women to visit Badel, a tiny village in eastern Nepal.

Throughout her career, Olds has learned to follow her own interests and not simply write about "saleable" topics. You, too, will write better about issues in which you're personally involved or invested. If you continue writing about the topics you really love, you'll be on your way to developing a specialty—which increases your appeal to editors, who'll think of you when they need an article in your area of expertise.

Even if you think you're doing everything right, Olds advises, be prepared to deal with rejections. Don't take them personally; they don't mean you're terrible. They just mean that the item you submitted is not suitable for this particular market at this particular time. Some writers, including Olds, have on occasion earned more money selling a piece that had originally been rejected than the original publication would have paid. In her opinion, selling well is the best revenge.

Sometimes rejection letters offer hidden encouragement—when you get an individually addressed note of rejection, you're coming up in the world (over the form rejection slip). When the note contains words of advice, consider them seriously; they may help you improve your work. And when a rejection note invites you to submit future work, seize the opportunity quickly. This editor likes something about your writing, so act on this expression of confidence—and do it fast. Editors move quickly from one publication to another. When you find one who's on your side, it's wise to develop your relationship.

Nina Zipkin

Nina Zipkin's mom urged her to pick a new activity when she entered eighth grade at her school in Connecticut. Nina chose the school newspaper, and soon found herself writing about fashion and movies—two of her favorite pastimes. The newspaper's faculty advisor was so impressed with Nina's work that she was the staffer chosen to interview the school's principal when he retired. Her story ran on page one.

As the school year was winding down, Nina put together some of her clips and went to the high school she would be attending in the autumn. She visited the high school newspaper office, and talked to a number of the student staff members. She was invited to check back at the end of the summer to help put together the back-to-school issue of the paper. Unlike a lot of freshmen, she realized, she would start high school already involved in an activity with a number of sophomores, juniors, and seniors.

But Nina was not satisfied with writing only for the school paper. After working as an umpire and scorekeeper for younger girls' softball games, she decided to apply to her twice-weekly town newspaper for one of the jobs that pays high school students to report on local games.

Nina may or may not pursue writing as a career someday, but for now it's helping open doors for her and get her involved in school and the community—and it may eventually earn her some spending money, too.

. 1 0 .

MANAGING YOUR
WRITING CAREER

FOR MOST TEENAGERS, and for most authors generally, writing is more like a serious hobby than a business—something they do because they like to write rather than because they need to pay the bills. But some people want more. They want to make money, and maybe even pursue a career in writing.

There's no need for you to decide now that you want to be a full-time professional writer someday. But there are ways you can open that door for yourself, even if you never walk through it. And even if you see your writing as never being more than something you do on the side, there are some ways to manage your writing "career" so you get the most out of it.

First, get organized. Keep lists of stories you've done, and stories you want to do. Keep lists of markets—publications you've written for, or would like to write for. Make yet another list for matches, when a story idea seems perfect for a particular market. Sometimes Tim creates a grid: story ideas along the top, magazines down the side, and then notes when a story idea was sent to the corresponding magazine. If it's rejected, he goes to the next magazine on the list. (Submitting the same story to one or more magazines at once can be touchy. Some magazines don't like it, some don't care. It's good to check a magazine's "simultaneous submissions" policy beforehand, and it's always a good idea to let an editor know if the idea is on another editor's desk at the same time.)

Tim keeps a list of every story idea he proposes to magazines, and notes whether it was accepted or rejected. If accepted, he notes when it's due, how many words it should be, and how much he's going to get paid. He enters the date that he sends in the story, and the date that the magazine confirms receipt. He notes the date when the magazine tells him the story has been accepted, and then when he receives the check.

Develop your own system for collecting and keeping track of story ideas. Some writers use an old-fashioned phrase—"gathering string"—for the process of collecting clippings or tidbits of information on a topic. Both Tim and Lizzie have story ideas that they're not ready to write yet for one reason or another. But when they come across something—an article, a quote, a factoid—that might be in the story they might write someday, they clip it out or scribble it down and stick it into a file folder. Eventually the idea ripens; they realize they've got enough information to do a story or, more likely, something happens to serve as a "hook" so that the story is trendy or timely. For example, for a couple of years Tim built a file on kids' etiquette and ethics on the Web. He decided the story was ready to pitch when a New Jersey high school valedictorian got into trouble over Web ethics. She had been admitted to Harvard, but the university withdrew its acceptance when it came to light that the girl had "borrowed" material from the Web—plagiarized, in other words—for the column she wrote for her local newspaper. That little news story gave Tim the "hook" he was looking for to introduce the story to editors as a larger examination of how many kids—and their parents—don't know or ignore legal and ethical standards when they're using the Internet. The editors at *Sky*, Delta's in-flight magazine, snapped up the story.

We've described story ideas as a writer's natural resources. Ideas, and completed stories, are also a writer's inventory. Once you've done a story, you can sell it again and again, sometimes as a reprint, or sometimes as what writers call a re-slant. They use much of the same material and research to do a different version of the story, sometimes for a different audience. Let's say you have your temporary driver's permit, and your folks put you behind the wheel on a family vacation to Yellowstone National Park. (Tim actually did this with Lizzie, except in Grand Canyon National Park. He doesn't recommend it for the faint-hearted; there were a number of white-knuckle turns on those narrow mountain roads overlooking steep drop-offs.)

What can you do with that? Well, you can write something for a blog, of course. And for the school paper. You can also write something for an auto magazine, like one of the American Automobile Association publications, with the focus on how great it was as a kid to learn to drive on a family vacation. You can write something for a parenting magazine with tips for parents on teaching a kid to drive from the kid's point of view. You can also do a straight travel piece for a newspaper or magazine on what a family can do or see while tooling around Yellowstone.

Keep track of what you make and what you spend. You might need to know your writing income for tax purposes or for college financial aid forms. Having itemized expenses can also come in handy for tax purposes, if you earn enough that you have to pay taxes. In that case, sometimes your expenses—everything from the cost of your pen to putting gas in the car to get to an interview—may be deductible as a business expense. But don't take our word for any of this. If you have any questions at all about finances and taxes, ask your parents or their tax advisor.

Aside from the nuts and bolts of career management, think about the larger issues of what you want to write and for whom. Keep your goals in mind, and keep thinking about how to make them happen. Keep thinking about ways you can improve different aspects of your writing, from finding ideas to doing research to the actual writing. Take a class in shorthand to help speed up your notetaking. Try some creative writing exercises. Read a newspaper or magazine story and imagine how you might re-tell it as a narrative, in chronological order, or how you might present it as a TV show or movie. Work on your craft. Take writing classes and courses. Maybe you have no interest in writing a screenplay, but many writers say that taking a screenwriting workshop has helped them shape their books and articles, and give them pace and drama. Listen to good interviews on television and radio (we like Terri Gross on National Public Radio's "Fresh Air"). If you are intent on getting seriously into freelancing for money, join Freelance Success (www.freelancesuccess.com), and take advantage of the tips and advice shared by other writers both in the group's newsletter and in its online forum.

Be wary of taking steps backward or sideways. One of Tim's students at the Graduate School of Journalism at Columbia University asked if he could miss a class to attend a one-day writing workshop. Tim has granted this sort of request at times in the past, but this time he said no. The student had been writing extensively for publications aimed at college students, and that's what the workshop was about. Tim said the student was already established in that area of writing; if the workshop had been focused on an area the student wanted to get into, such as science writing or writing long-form narratives, Tim probably would have said yes.

Once you're known as writer, people will come to you and present opportunities for you to write. You have to look at these requests on a case-by-case basis, of course, but don't do something just because you've been asked. If you are trying to be a professional writer, then people should pay you for your writing. Let's say you have a neighbor who is a doctor. She asks you to look over her annual holiday letter to check it for mistakes and to make any suggestions for how it could be written more smoothly. Is that something you should do without being paid? Would you ask the doctor to give you a physical for free?

Many publications that accept submissions from teenagers, especially those on the Web, do not pay writers for the articles they publish. We think writers should always be paid, but that's not practical in many cases. And besides, sometimes merely being published is enough, especially for young writers just starting out. But once you get more established, be wary of anybody who wants to publish your work for free and tells you that it will be good exposure. People die of exposure. In any situation where you won't get paid, look carefully at the publication. Is anybody getting paid? Are the editors making money? Are advertisements being sold? Is the printer being paid? If there's money anywhere in the equation, perhaps some of it should go to the writers, the people who are providing the whole reason that readers pick up the publication in the first place.

Protect your legal rights, especially your copyrights. First, of course, it helps to know what can and cannot be copyrighted. Characters cannot be copyrighted. Titles cannot be copyrighted. Ideas cannot be copyrighted. All that can be copyrighted is the presentation, the actual writing. Many novice writers think they have to formally copyright their work. In truth, anything you write is protected by copyright the moment you set it down on paper or on a screen. You don't even need to put "Copyright by" or the © symbol, but of course you can if you wish, especially at the start of the book or article. (Some people stick a copyright notice on every page, and that looks amateurish.) If and when you write something that is published, you are granting the publication the right to publish. Tim and many other professional writers do register their articles with the federal government (www.copyright.gov), but they typically do it after publication. The main advantage is that if someone does violate the copyright—such as by posting the article on a Web site without permission—it is easier to obtain damages. Tim has made thousands of dollars by keeping track of stories reprinted without his permission and sending letters to the offenders informing them that they are violating his copyright and that they owe him a certain amount of money, which is usually whatever he would have charged them for the reprint if they had asked.

This is important: When you agree to let someone publish your work, be aware of what rights you are granting or giving up. Some publications will want you to sign something saying that you are surrendering "all rights" to the work. Avoid this if you can. It not only means that the publication can reprint and resell your work, but that you cannot. If you give up all rights, technically you can't even make photocopies of the article to send to relatives or post the article on your own Web site. Retain as many rights as you can. Ask, and negotiate. If a publication wants to print your story, ask for more money if the story is also going to be on the publication's Web site. Make sure that if the publication sells reprint rights, you get some of the money. The same for movie rights; Hollywood is buying more and more magazine articles for possible movies, and it would be a shame for your article to become a movie and for you not to get any of the credit or money.

Tim Says:
ORGANIZE

Writers, especially novices, too often overlook structure. They get an idea, they do some research, and they sit down at the keyboard and start pounding away. Too often—and too late—they find that the story is jumbled, that it doesn't flow, that it seems to have "holes." They need to get better organized and spend more time on story structure.

Some people use outlines. I make lists. A list of what I need in the story: for example, someone who is on one side of the issue, someone who is on the other, someone who has mixed feelings, a report that has the latest statistics, someone who is an authority. That sort of thing. Then I make sure I have the people and numbers and facts that are required to tell the whole story from every angle.

How do you know when you've completed your research? Well, you never really do, but too many young writers skimp on the research and reporting. They're too eager to start writing. In truth, the more research you do—and the more organizing before you start writing—the easier the writing is. Sometimes you know you've got enough research when you stop seeing and hearing anything new, when people are repeating what others have said. Most of the time, if you have a deadline, you don't stop researching until you absolutely have to start writing to meet the deadline.

When my research is finished, I make more lists, starting with the most important aspects of the story, the big building blocks. Then I go through my notes and research and fill in the details under the big building blocks. I pay a lot of attention to transitions—the use of language to move the story from one main aspect to another. Sometimes I'll juggle the order of the big building blocks, the main aspects of the story, in order to make an easier, smoother transition from one main point to another.

It's difficult to do, but try to remember: The more time you spend on research and organizing, the easier—and better—the writing will be.

• A LONGER GLANCE AT A YOUNG WRITER •

Lindsay Crudele

Lindsay Crudele credits her parents with instilling in her an early love of reading, which she believes led her to become a published writer at an age when a lot of kids are still learning to read. Her mother, a receptionist, and father, a high school English teacher, "always encouraged me to read, and they took me to the library a lot," she said. "As a result, I never saw the library as this sort of nerdy place . . . the librarians, I remember, really made stories come alive. I didn't think of writing as a chore; it was just something I knew how to do."

Her first taste of publishing success growing up in Rhode Island came in kindergarten, when she entered—and won—a story contest in the *Providence Journal* with an original short story she'd written featuring animals, instead of humans, as the main characters. Her story was published in the *Journal*'s Junior Edition section; she was four. A few years later, when she was in the fourth grade at a Cranston public school, she saw a small notice on the *Journal*'s Kid's Beat page looking for young writers. For the required writing sample, she sent in an essay she'd written on President George H. W. Bush's refusal to sign an environmental treaty at a conference in Rio de Janeiro. That piece, which she later admitted was "a tirade against Bush," won her the first of many *Journal* assignments she would receive. Her mission was to spend the night at the local zoo and then write an article on her behind-the-scenes experience. For the occasion, Crudele wore a black bowler-style hat "that I thought was reporterly."

The resulting article from that first assignment went over well at the *Journal,* and she continued to write for the paper as a sort of junior reporter (although she eventually ditched the bowler). "I continuously called my editor to propose ideas, and even though he'd reject about half of them, that's how I kept getting assignments," Crudele remembered. As she was published more and more, adults would recognize her newspaper byline and give her other ideas to pitch. "They would tell me about some interesting person or interesting place that I could write about, so I'd pass it on to my editor and sometimes I got to write those stories," she said.

Being a kid who could write, not even a teenager yet, led to some interesting opportunities. Like the summer she was ten, when she wrote a series of articles for the *Journal* on fun things for kids to do in Rhode Island. "I basically pored over guidebooks and phone books, looking for interesting activities . . . Rhode Island is small, but it's a rich state for writers," Crudele said. One of her favorite assignments from that summer was reviewing all of Rhode Island's water parks. There are three. However, she and her family made it a "grand tour."

Perhaps the most important thing Crudele learned from that summer of constantly pitching ideas, even though many of them were rejected, was that "knowing your publication and constantly generating ideas is crucial to show that you have an interest and you're motivated and ready to work."

Some of her other successful pitches included an interview with the children's author Avi and an article on pigeon clubs, inspired by finding a lost pigeon with a tag on its foot. When Crudele was eleven, the National Governors' Association Convention was held in Rhode Island, and through her writing connections she was able to get a job working there. This led to meeting Rhode Island's governor and state poet laureate, an experience she described as "amazing."

Crudele eventually moved on to bigger and better sections of the *Journal.* After getting an assignment from the education section, she struck up a relationship with the Metro editor and continued to write for the *Journal* through middle school and high school. During the summers, she would intern at various area papers, including the *Cranston Herald* and *Warwick Beacon.*

One strategy she used, often successfully, to find jobs or internships was job shadowing. She would call an editor, for example, and ask if she could shadow him or her for a day to experience firsthand what an editor does and how a paper works. Most adults she asked were happy to help, and when she met them she'd bring along a book of all her newspaper clips from publications including the *Journal,* the *Parents Paper, Rhode Island Monthly,* and *National Geographic World.* On one occasion, her host was so impressed that he offered her a summer internship on the spot. Crudele, recognizing the value of her clips, kept them in a leather portfolio (purchased at an art supply store) so that they'd be portable for going to meetings.

Along with shadowing adults you admire, Crudele advises young writers to "overestimate yourself—act like you're a real hotshot" to bolster your own confidence so that editors will trust you. Of course, even young hotshots make mistakes. One of her biggest regrets is not backing up her work enough with hard copies or on disks. Crudele learned this lesson the hard way after graduating from college. In the summer of 2003 she was working as a producer at Boston public radio station WBUR when a computer holding "absolutely the best work of my career"—a lengthy narrative journalism piece on how residents of Boston's North End view their neighborhood's changing demographics and character—was stolen.

Even after a setback, whether it's as small as a rejection letter or as big as a stolen computer, Crudele's strongest advice for young writers is to keep reading and writing. Activities such as keeping a journal, writing poetry, or joining a speech and debate club will help your communication skills. She especially recommended keeping a "fragment journal" to jot down fragments of ideas whenever they hit you. "Just write as much as humanly possible," she concluded.

BOOKS:

Is There One in You?

ONE OF TIM'S favorite quotes is, "Times are bad. Children no longer obey their parents, and everyone is writing a book." Sometimes he uses it when speaking to writers' groups, and asks the writers to guess who said it. Nobody has ever guessed right: the quote is attributed to Marcus Tullius Cicero, the ancient Roman statesman, orator, and writer, and it just goes to show that some things haven't changed all that much in two thousand years. Except that maybe even more people are writing books, from CEOs to lots of retired grandmas and grandpas to Paris Hilton's little dog Tinkerbell. Writing a book is hard, even when the material is right in front of you. Don't pick a topic that will present difficulties in gathering material, or the right kind of good material for a book. It seems as if teenagers have had the most luck in recent years writing two types of books: fantasies, and this-is-my-life stories. The personal stories can be nonfiction memoirs, or they can be fictionalized stories based on the author's real experiences and feelings. In either case, and indeed no matter what you write, remember that you have to tell a story. A good story that moves along, with interesting characters whom readers have feelings about one way or the other, with goals that the central character is trying to achieve, and with obstacles that the hero has to overcome.

There may be lots of things that keep you from writing a book, but lack of interest in the topic should never be a reason. Remember what we said previously about finding ideas and choosing subjects to write about? It always helps if it's something you care about. (When people ask what Tim writes about, Lizzie's mom Nancy sometimes tells them, "He writes about whatever he's interested in, or people pay him enough to *get* interested in.") Well, if you should be interested in an article topic, you should be even more passionate about the subject of any book you undertake. It makes sense. A book is a huge project that will take an unbelievable amount of work over a period of months or maybe years. As Benjamin Disraeli, the statesman and former English prime minister, said, "The best way to get acquainted with a subject is to write a book about it." You'll do more than just get acquainted with your subject— you're going to get tired of it, maybe even sick of it. Just don't get bored with it. Once you lose interest, it's very difficult to finish, and even harder to do a good job. Why invest so much of yourself—so much time, energy, and in most cases heart—into something that might become drudgery?

Once you have settled on the story you want to tell in a book, be aware that the odds are long on getting published. Tim tells his editorial and publishing clients that the chances of any single book idea actually getting published is probably one in a thousand. They express shock, and he then tells them he's probably exaggerating; the odds are probably more like one in ten thousand. Someone once told him about a study that showed that even among experienced professional writers like himself, people who have had lots of their work published, the odds against seeing a book idea actually become a book are four hundred to one. That said, a lot of people are beating the odds. There are something like eighty thousand books published in the United States in a given year, and that number is rising rapidly, largely because new self-publishing and print-on-demand technology is making it easier and cheaper for anyone to publish his or her book. But we'll talk more later about self-publishing, and its particular appeal for teenagers. First, let's talk about how traditional publishing works.

If your first book is fiction or poetry, you'll probably have to write the entire book to get a publisher to consider it. Poetry is typically submitted directly to a publishing house, which usually specializes in poetry and therefore is small and poor and doesn't pay much money up front, if any, to the poet. In truth, most poets don't seem to mind. They're not in it for the money. Getting a book of poems published can be enough of a thrill, especially if the poet is an academic and getting a book published helps his or her university or college career. Novelists also often submit complete books to publishers, both large and small, but it's almost always preferable to have an agent; many publishers, especially at big houses, prefer to receive manuscripts from agents rather than from authors directly. Unfortunately, there's a classic Catch-22: it's difficult to get published without an agent, and at the same time it's difficult to get an agent unless you've been published. If you submit a manuscript on your own, it often lands on a "slush pile" at the publishing house with other unsolicited manuscripts. It will be read—or, at least, looked at briefly—by someone, eventually, but that someone will most likely be an editorial assistant who is not long out of college and may be only a few years older than you are. The odds are against it, but it does happen: occasionally a particularly bright and discerning and persuasive young assistant will take a liking to a manuscript and actually read it all the way through. The assistant then hands it up to a more senior editor, and if that editor likes it and hands it up, and that editor likes it, eventually the manuscript is considered by either a single person or a group of people who have the final authority to make a decision. In a small house this may well be one person, the publisher whose name is probably on the door (and the imprint). In a big publishing house, final authority may rest with a publishing committee that includes not only the publisher but various editors, marketing people, publicists, accountants, lawyers, and others. Many factors are considered by the publisher or the committee. Is it a good book? Of course it is; otherwise it wouldn't have gotten that far in the process. But many, many, many good books never get published. Much more important to a committee at a big house is the answer to this question: Will this book make money? Marketing people talk about who will buy the book: is there a natural audience for it, a demographic profile? In the fiction world, publishers try to capitalize on the success of other recent novels, and publish books that are similar. Other important factors are how well the author can help publicize the book. Does he or she have any media connections? Is he or she good on television and radio? One of the things an agent or an editor will want to know is whether you have a "platform." In other words, do you have some sort of public persona or public arena that will draw people to you and create interest in what you have to say—as if, literally, you were up on a platform to speak to people? Maybe you've been a student activist. Maybe you have a local newspaper column with a loyal readership. Maybe you're the student member of the local school board, or the youth leader of the local gun club. Maybe you're the person that the local TV station always turns to for comment on vegetarianism or ethical treatment of animals or what it's like to be a young Republican.

The process of getting published is different for nonfiction books, which are typically easier for authors to sell to publishers. Most experienced nonfiction authors do not write the entire book first. Instead, they produce a proposal. There are a number of good how-to books that offer advice and models for nonfiction book proposals, including one that Tim edited for the American Society of Journalists and Authors: *The ASJA Guide to Freelance Writing*. Essentially, a typical book proposal includes a pitch that summarizes the book; a marketing plan that describes who will buy the book and why, often in great detail and backed up by statistics; a chapter outline, with summaries of each chapter; and one or more sample chapters, usually including chapter one. A committee at a big publishing house has the same bottom-line considerations for nonfiction as fiction: what are the chances that this book will make money for the company? The proposal should be a fair representation of what the book is going to be about, but first and foremost the proposal is a selling document. You are using it to sell your idea, your book—and most important, yourself—to the publishing house.

Nonfiction authors sometimes send their proposals directly to publishers—especially smaller publishers—but almost all authors, both fiction and non, prefer to work with an agent if they can get one. How do you get an agent? None of this—sigh—is easy. Of course if it were easy, everybody, as Cicero said, would not only be writing a book, but getting it published. Again, there are a number of books that describe how to find an agent—the right agent—including two by author-friendly agents: *Jeff Herman's Guide to Book Publishers, Editors and Literary Agents* and Michael Larsen's *Literary Agents: What They Do, How They Do It, and How to Find and Work with the Right One for You*. There are other guidebooks describing various agents, and would-be authors often spend a lot of time poring over those lists looking for agents who specialize in whatever their book is about. One of the best ways of finding an agent, however, is to look at books that you admire and/or books that are similar to yours in some way, books that would attract similar readers—and similar publishers. In the acknowledgments, authors typically thank their agents. Take down the agent's name, look up his or her contact details, and get in touch. Tell the agent you have a book that is similar in some ways, and might be of interest to the agent—and publishers—for the same reasons as the other book.

Here is something very important, a trap that many young first-time writers fall into. Never pay an agent a reading fee. Never pay an agent anything up front. Some disreputable "agents" want reading fees in the hundreds of dollars, and promise that they will make suggestions to help you get your book or your proposal in shape so they can submit it to publishers. Rubbish. They're probably pocketing your fees and doing very little for you. Reputable agents, the kind of agents you want to deal with, do not charge reading fees.

Of course you want to meet prospective agents face to face if you can, but if you can't it's no big deal. Many authors have long and profitable relationships with agents whom they rarely, if ever, lay eyes on, especially authors who live elsewhere in the country but have an agent in New York. And while it may seem obvious to try to get the most high-powered agent you can, many authors—especially those just starting out—are more comfortable with agents who don't have a lot of celebrity-author clients and are perhaps more willing and available to spend time working on their books rather than running interference for celebrities.

Suppose you're in the enviable position of having more

than one agent interested in your book. How do you choose which one represents you? There's no easy answer, except to say you should choose the one that you're most comfortable with, the one you think will do the best job for the book, and the one who is most enthusiastic—but realistic—about the book and best understands both the book and you the author. Most agents have written agreements with their clients (if you're not eighteen, your parents might have to sign for you) that specify how much commission the agent will get—typically 15 percent for most of the book's potential earnings—and what expenses the author will or won't be required to pay, such as photocopying and postage for preparing and delivering the proposal to publishers. The agreement with the agent should include some sort of time limit so that you are free to look for a new agent if the proposal doesn't sell.

The agent may have you rework the proposal. It's okay to resist this a bit, especially if you disagree with some of the changes, but remember that the agent is the expert, and it's that expertise that earns commissions. The agent has a stake in getting your book published; otherwise he or she doesn't get paid. The agent should keep you informed, but don't expect a lot of hand-holding. Don't bug the agent with lots of phone calls or e-mails, and don't expect regular lunches with your agent (unless it looks like you're going to have a bestseller and a movie deal; then your agent will have all the time in the world for you). On the other hand, if your agent is totally unresponsive, doesn't keep you updated, and won't answer your occasional calls and messages, it might be time to fire him or her. Don't do this lightly, because other agents are justifiably leery of a client with a history of dumping agents. At the same time, all agents know that some of their colleagues take on clients they shouldn't have taken on in the first place, and that a split is often best for both author and agent.

In a perfect world, the agent shows your manuscript or proposal to publishers, they shout, "This is great! I've got to publish this kid!" and they get in an auction to see who will pay you the most to publish your book. Alas, the world is rarely perfect. If you get any advance at all you're probably doing pretty well, though some teenagers—see our "Glance" at Zoe Trope, who got a six-figure advance—do make serious money. Publishers enter into contracts with authors to pay them royalties—a percentage of the money that the book earns. This can be based on the list price of the book, or the net earnings of the publisher, or something in between. It can be a couple of percentage points or it can be 15 percent or it can be something in between, with a scale that slides according to sales. Either way, few authors ever get royalties beyond the advance that the publisher pays up front—the advance against royalties. If you get a five-thousand-dollar advance for example (hooray!), that means the publisher has to sell enough books to pay you five thousand dollars in royalties before you get another dollar.

If you don't get an agent or don't find a big publisher willing to put your book out, don't worry, you're among millions. You don't need to give up. Try smaller publishing houses or university presses. Many young people, like another of our "Glance" subjects, Marty Beckerman, got their first books into print by self-publishing. Years ago there was a certain stigma to self-publishing, especially among "vanity" presses that charged authors dearly and sold them stacks of books that ended up moldering in garages and basements. In recent years, however, new print-on-demand (POD) technology has changed the economics of self-publishing and has made it economically feasible for publishers such as iUniverse, Xlibris, AuthorHouse, and others to help authors get their books into print. Authors no longer have to pay thousands of dollars for hundreds of books; instead, they can pay relatively little, and the publisher prints a book when someone orders it and pays for it. Tim has gotten involved in POD in a small way, and is a partner in the first self-publishing system in a U.S. bookstore. Called BooksBy-Bookends (more information at www.booksbybookends.com), it's perhaps the fastest and cheapest self-publishing option for most people, and many students and teachers have used it to get books, including collections of stories, into book form.

One caution about self-publishing: be prepared to do your own marketing, and maybe your own distribution. Some POD houses will help get your book listed at online bookstores, or you can do that yourself, but it is rare for the big bookstore chains to stock POD books. A better bet is your local independent bookstore, if you have one. Offer to do a signing or give a talk about how you wrote your book and self-published, and how others can do it, too. You won't have any of the support—distribution, sales people, publicists, advertising, and so on—that you would have had if a big publisher had picked your book. On the other hand, if you do manage to sell some books, the royalties for POD books are typically higher, often twice or more as high, as those offered by commercial publishers.

And just because you've self-published, that doesn't mean you've given up the chance to become a best-selling author. While publishing houses generally express disdain for self-publishing—after all, self-published books compete with the books they put out—they are becoming increasingly aware of the potential of some self-published books. A growing number of self-published books are being picked up by big publishing houses, which then throw their marketing and distribution muscle behind them. In some ways, an author who publishes his or her own book makes it easier for a commercial publisher; if you get your book printed and sell one thousand copies yourself, that tells a publisher that there may well indeed be a national market for your book—and that's what those committees are always looking for.

To conclude this discussion of books, let's go back to the beginning of the process. When you've decided you want to write a book, ask yourself, "Why do I want to do this? How do I think writing a book will change my life?" If the main reasons for doing a book are to get rich and famous, forget it. You are almost surely going to be disappointed. But if you want to write a book because there's a story you *need* to tell, if you are looking forward to the process and what you'll learn from it, you may well find that writing a book—whether it ends up atop the Amazon listings or stashed in the bottom of a drawer somewhere—is an extremely rewarding and satisfying experience.

Lizzie Says:
SEEK OUT CRITICISM

Most people don't like being criticized, and try to avoid criticism. Serious writers, however, often go looking for it. It's part of improving and growing as a writer. You need to be able to critique your own work, and to find people who will help you critique it. Too many writers fall in love with their words. They think something they've written sounds wonderful primarily because they wrote it. And so do their loved ones, their friends and parents. Beginning writers typically say, "Well, everybody I've showed it to said it was really good." Of course. They've shown it to their friends and relatives, people who love them. The test is when they show their writing to someone who doesn't love them, someone who has only a few minutes to read, like most of us, and wants to read something really good during those few minutes.

Try various friends to see who will give you an honest opinion. Maybe you can get a small group of people together—they don't have to be friends, they merely need to be interested in writing—to comment on each other's writing. Sometimes English or journalism or other teachers will read and critique your work if you ask nicely. Maybe you or your parents know someone who is a writer and might be willing to look at your stuff. You want honesty and candor, not cruelty or picky comments. Constructive criticism will help you improve your writing. Don't despair if someone finds lots of errors or mistakes. You don't need to accept all of them. But try to learn from every bit of criticism, whether or not it's fair or accurate. And when you're reading other people's writing, remember to give them the same sort of constructive criticism that you'd like to receive.

SOCCER DREAMS:
A FAMILY PROJECT

It just didn't seem right. Twelve-year-old Leah Lauber had achieved her dream of watching the U.S. Women's National Soccer Team win the 1999 FIFA Women's World Cup, but she couldn't find a publisher for the book she'd written about the experience. Publisher after publisher rejected it. But after all her work recording and writing the story, Leah couldn't let it go. Eventually it became a family project, and the Laubers, of St. Petersburg, Florida, published it themselves.

Leah's adventure began in the spring of 1998 when she applied, and was accepted, to the X-Press Team, the kids' section of the *St. Petersburg Times*. She was soon a junior reporter for the paper, covering new movies, concerts, and, most enthusiastically, soccer.

As a member of the X-Team, Leah was able to combine her

two passions: writing and soccer. She wrote about her own team's progress as well as her experiences watching the U.S. Women's National team and meeting some of its members. At clinics and after games she was sometimes able to interview her heroes. With this on-the-job reporting experience, she wrote five features on women's soccer for the X-Press section.

But Leah's biggest thrill came when she won a soccer photography contest sponsored by Hewlett-Packard. The prize was a trip for her whole family to the Rose Bowl in Pasadena, California, for the 1999 Women's World Cup Finals. When the U.S. team beat the Chinese team in the finals to win the World Cup, it was a dream come true for Leah—"That was the greatest time," she wrote in *Soccer Dreams,* her subsequent book about the experience, "seeing my heroes enjoy the highlights of their careers."

Leah's own writing career, on the other hand, was shaky getting off the ground. With a stack of rejection letters and without a publisher signed on to release her book, the Lauber family was ready to give up on it. However, the project got a second chance when it was announced that the 2003 Women's World Cup would be moved back to the United States because of the SARS epidemic in China, its planned site. The Laubers realized that increased publicity for women's soccer could translate into more attention for Leah's book, so they decided to publish it themselves.

Soccer Dreams became a family endeavor. Leah had already written the text and taken some of the photographs; her father, Chris, a professional sports photographer, provided all but four of the book's remaining pictures. Her mother, Rya, came up with the cover and overall design (as well as the book's title), while her younger sister, Nicole, and grandmother, Pat, transcribed the tapes of interviews Leah had conducted with nearly every U.S. National Team member. In addition, her dad helped by scanning and laying out the photos. Even her grandfather contributed to the effort with pictures he'd shot of Leah with team members in 1997. Her grandmother and both parents also shared editing and general consulting duties.

The initial, self-published print run of *Soccer Dreams* was about 2,600 copies. The production cost per book came to about $4.51—fairly high, but as the Laubers see it, a worthy investment. As women's soccer becomes more popular, people will buy more books about it. Leah's story, reflecting the spirit and perseverance of both its author and the players she followed, appeals to every audience.

And who knows? *Soccer Dreams,* currently available at some soccer supply stores, www.amazon.com and www.soccer dreamsbook.com, may be the key that unlocks the door to Leah's next adventure.

THIS BOOK:
How We Did It

WELL, we've done it. We've written a book together. Obviously we did some things right along the way, but we've had a few bumps in the road, too. Tim is a seasoned author, so the process is nothing new to him, but for first-timer Lizzie there were a few surprises. Her previous publishing experience was mostly limited to e-mailing articles to editors, so this was a big step. Here's how we did it:

Before this project, Tim was the editor of a book on freelance writing put out by the American Society of Journalists and Authors (ASJA) and published by St. Martin's Press. Tim's editor at St. Martin's, Marian Lizzi, had developed a specialty in how-to books, ranging from self-help to cookbooks to a book on the history of funk music. During the process of working on the ASJA book, Tim mentioned to Marian that his own daughter, then seventeen years old, was also an aspiring writer. Marian saw the potential for a father-daughter writing team and proposed that the two do a book together on how teenagers can get published.

We both liked the idea from the beginning, but each of us had reservations. To Lizzie, the question was how much time this project would require. When we first started throwing the idea around, she was still a first-semester high-school senior, busy applying to colleges, keeping up with advanced placement work for her high school classes, and working a couple of part-time jobs after school.

"If I'm still this busy later in the year, I don't think I'm going to have time for this book," she told Tim. "There's too much writing in my life anyway, with college essays, school papers, and my column. I don't think I can do it."

Eventually, Tim convinced Lizzie otherwise by assuring her that once the college application process was over and high school had calmed down—even after high school ended—there would be lots of free time for writing. Luckily, he was right. By the time we actually started writing the book, Lizzie had been admitted to Oberlin College, had stopped writing the "High School Beat" column, and had practically finished high school. The only things she had left to write were messages in her friends' yearbooks.

Tim, on the other hand, had qualms of his own. He's already a comfortably established writer—why should he spend time writing a book like this when he could use it more profitably doing something else? As a novice writer, Lizzie stood to gain more financially and professionally than Tim from the project. Out of a mix of paternal duty and the desire to help Lizzie become an author, he did it anyway. It's actually worked out well, becoming a common bond for us to share during Lizzie's last summer in Ridgewood before leaving for college.

Back to the process: winter of Lizzie's senior year. Once we'd decided to take on the project, we had to convince St. Martin's Press that we could do it. Marian had only suggested the idea—she and her bosses hadn't formally accepted it yet. To get the contract, we had to submit a proposal. In this case, the proposal consisted of a pitch letter (explaining the concept of the book and why it would be a good buy for St. Martin's), a sample chapter and outline of the other chapters, a marketing plan (who will buy the book? why?), and a few writing samples by each of us. Tim, as the more experienced member of the team, wrote most of the proposal. Lizzie helped with ideas and editing.

We started with lists: why should kids get published? It's good experience, it's rewarding, it looks good on college applications, it can lead to more assignments, and so on. We brainstormed and scoured the Internet to think of the places, obscure as well as obvious, where young writers can be published. Perhaps the hardest (but most enjoyable) list to make was of random tips for teen writers, culled from our own publishing experiences.

Lizzie used her insider's knowledge of high school papers for inspiration, as well as experiences from her stint as a high school columnist and occasional contributor to our regional paper's Op-Ed page. She provided the firsthand insights about what it's like to be a young writer today. Tim drew from his years of writing experience, both working for eleven years as an Associated Press national writer and working for himself as a freelance writer for more than two decades, to describe the writing business in general, and to offer more long-range professional advice.

We submitted the proposal and it was accepted by St. Martin's. We negotiated our advance, then signed a contract that laid out specifics such as how long the book would be and our deadline for turning it in. (The timing was such that Lizzie's first legal contract she signed after turning eighteen was a book deal.) Marian wanted to meet Lizzie, so she invited her to an old-fashioned publishing lunch (without the martinis) in Manhattan. Lizzie took off part of the school day to take the train into the city, giving her teachers a note saying she had to have lunch with her editor.

We should have gone to work right away, even though our deadline—months away—seemed like it provided us all the time in the world. In those first weeks, though, mostly we thought and talked about what we should do. We procrastinated on actually doing the research and writing. Finally, when we realized we were both going to have to work hard to meet the deadline, we buckled down.

Our first scheduled meeting was literally a wake-up call. It was the first Monday of Lizzie's summer vacation, and after a long week of seemingly endless graduation celebrations, she wasn't exactly in the mood for waking up at 9 A.M. to work.

Nevertheless, Tim prevailed—"We've got to write this thing!"—and we held the first of many book meetings. The first one was probably the most formal: Tim and Lizzie went over the book's outline together, dividing up tasks and figuring out who would write each section.

Lizzie mostly took on the more general chapters—getting started as a writer, how to find ideas—as well as ones she could write from experience, like the section about school newspapers. She also contacted and/or interviewed adults who deal with young writers, like editors at the local paper and others she has written for. Tim covered the more detailed subjects, like how to actually propose and submit work for publication. When one of us finished a section, we'd show it to the other for edits, suggestions, corrections, and an overall review. Because we went over everything together before finalizing it, the book really is a joint effort. There's nothing in here that one of us wrote without input from the other.

As we made progress, meetings became less frequent and more productive. They often took place after meals, while we sat around the table feeling the pull of work from the upstairs office, still wanting to sit and talk for a few minutes. Once or twice a week, we broke the monotony of the daily routine with breakfast out at a local diner. We'd update each other on accomplishments—"I did a thousand words of chapter three and made some notes for more at the bottom; can you look at it?"—and things still to be done—"My interview forgot to call *again*." We'd also share good ideas, especially good people we found to talk to. When Tim got Lindsay Crudele's name from an acquaintance, Lizzie e-mailed her the next day to set up an interview. A few days later, she found Zoe Trope's LiveJournal, another lucky addition to our interview list. Interviews weren't the only ideas we picked up as we went along. In some cases, whole sections emerged (the one on writing coaches and mentors, for example) that weren't part of the original outline. The mini-profile of Lizzie's brother Jonny's minicareer as a writer was another one that we thought of midbook.

Even though we usually wrote separately, the entire process was cooperative. Before Lizzie conducted an interview, for instance (she did them all), she'd make up a list of questions and topics to discuss, then show it to Tim for his suggestions. If Tim came up with an idea for a new section, he and Lizzie talked about whether to include it, what should be in it, and where it would fit in the book. We both kept running lists of people still to contact and sections to write or edit, and fact-checked each other's work. After the first few days, Lizzie was working full-time in our house's third-floor converted-attic office, and Tim was working part-time on the book in addition to several other projects. One of the biggest surprises of the whole experience for Lizzie was how hard it is to work in an office all day, even if that office is really the top floor of your house. Sure, she'd heard people (okay, her parents) complain about it her whole life, but she never understood the potential for boredom and distraction in an office. Not to mention sunlight deprivation—she had to start taking lunch breaks in the backyard just to catch some rays.

The other big obstacle, at least for Lizzie, was managing her time so that there'd be enough for both work and play. Writing a book isn't easy, even when two people share the task. It requires long days of work that start with early mornings. And when you've stayed out too late the night before, Lizzie learned, it's difficult to concentrate on writing. Reluctant to give up her summer hangout time with friends before they scattered to colleges around the country, Lizzie disciplined herself to work hard from 9 to 5 (or 6, or 7) before heading out to relax with friends. And she learned that sometimes, it's okay to go home a little bit early if you need the sleep.

As the weeks passed and our project began to take shape, we decided that it would be helpful to have a paper copy of the evolving manuscript. Every section we drafted, complete or not, got printed out and compiled into our first rough copy of the book. With the whole thing on paper, it was easy to see which sections needed more work and which were already long enough—and how they were going to fit together. When we took off for a weekend near the end of July to go to a family reunion, it wasn't technically a weekend "off"—we brought the book. In the airport, on the plane, and even for a few hours over the weekend, we worked on marking it up with edits and suggestions. On Monday morning we were ready to get back to work, and we spent that week writing to fill in gaps or make transitions from one section to another. The last few days we spent reading, re-reading, and polishing, handing printouts back and forth, marking them up, and handing them back and forth again. On the day the manuscript was due to be turned in, as we write this, Tim is looking over Lizzie's shoulder as she goes through last-minute changes on the computer screen. When we finish this section on how we wrote the book, Lizzie will close the file, print a copy for each of us, and e-mail the manuscript off to our editor. As we were rounding into the home stretch of the book, Marian, our editor, called to tell us that she was leaving St. Martin's Press. This is not unusual in the publishing world; Tim has had a couple of books start under one editor and finish under another. This time, our book was taken over by another editor, Julie Mente, who had worked with Tim on a previous book. Lizzie didn't get another lunch—Julie was taking over other new books, and Lizzie was in crunch time on our book—but Julie turned out to be just as helpful and supportive as Marian had been.

All in all, it was a great project for us, a good and productive way for us to spend time together during Lizzie's last summer at home before going off to college. We had a handful of inevitable moments of impatience and frustration with each other, of course, but those passed quickly—usually when Tim realized that if Lizzie wasn't doing something the way he thought it should be done, it either was because he hadn't explained what he wanted or else Lizzie had a better idea in the first place.

The success of this book depends, in the end, on how readers such as you like the book, and how many people buy it and read it. But however the book is received, for us it has been a great collaboration.

THE LAST WORD

All right, you've gotten this far, so you must be pretty serious about writing and getting published. What now? Well, make a plan and set a goal. Better yet, make several plans and set several goals: large, small, short-term, long-term. Start thinking like a writer, and thinking of yourself as a writer, looking for stories and places where your writing can be published. Most of all, write. Write things you can send out to be published, and write things just for yourself. Try different styles and genres. Assume different voices. Try narratives. Use a lot of dialogue. Try writing a passage of pure description, maybe about your room or one of your friends. Set up a blog or a Web page of your own, and start by publishing yourself online. If you've got some good story ideas, start sending out queries. Get on the school paper, or apply for a job or internship at the newspaper in your town. Volunteer your services as a writer for a local charity, or to write up stories for the local paper about the youth sports leagues in your town.

Somehow, any way you can, every way you can, put yourself out there as a writer. That's the only way it will happen.

Resources for
Young Writers

HERE ARE a number of Web sites that may be helpful: some that offer advice for young writers, some that publish young writers, and some that do both. (Assume that a site doesn't pay unless we say so, but it never hurts to ask; sometimes policies change, and sometimes markets that don't pay most people will pay you.)

TEEN WRITING

www.thescriptorium.net/youth.html
The Scriptorium
An online resource center for young writers that features articles, interviews, book reviews, exercises, and an interactive workshop. Updated monthly.

www.teenwriting.about.com
Creative Writing for Teens
This site provides links, articles, exercises, and forums especially for teen writers. The site also has discussion groups to share your work.

www.wordcraftsmen.org
Wordcraftsmen
Wordcraftsmen, a site dedicated to publishing authors under thirty years old, publishes everything from news articles to short pieces of fiction. It also features online journals, forums, and Web links for young writers.

www.writersbbs.com
Writer's BBS
Writer's BBS is a community for all writers, not just young adults. It hosts more than fifty discussion/critique forums for all different genres, styles, and age groups.

www.girlything.com

Girly Thing

Girly Thing is an online magazine aimed at teen girls that features articles on fashion, beauty, and fitness. Monthly.

www.channelone.com

Channel One

Channel One News is a television news program shown to over 8.5 million students in middle and high schools across the country. ChannelOne.com, the Web component to the show, offers teens the chance to publish their own writing in the Student Showcase section.

www.fictionpress.com

FictionPress

This is a self-publishing online community (made up of forums, organized by topic) used mostly by teens to showcase their poems and stories. You'll find reviews for your work and other writing you can read and review.

www.teenink.com

TeenInk

TeenInk publishes teen poetry, essays, stories, and opinions by teenagers, both online and in print. They run contests and are well known for their books and magazines. Monthly.

www.merlynspen.org

Merlyn's Pen

Merlyn's Pen is a print magazine focused on publishing

young writers. They publish all genres, nearly all forms of writing in any length, and in any style. They also publish annual teen anthologies and post works online. Monthly.

www.ypp.net
Young People's Press
Young People's Press is a Web site that accepts nonfiction submissions from youth and young adults between the ages of fourteen and twenty-four. The work can be a feature story, opinion piece, first-person story, or profile of a youth making a difference.

www.teenworldnews.com
Teen World News
This Web site is dedicated to connecting teen writers across the globe. It publishes articles, poems, and stories on just about every teen-related topic. It's a place for teens to learn about news that affects them and to share ideas on everything from human rights to hot fashion trends.

www.tcr.org
The Concord Review
The Concord Review is the only scholarly journal in the world dedicated to publishing the work of high school/secondary students. They publish high-quality history research papers. Some sample essays are available on the site. Quarterly.

www.teenlit.com

TeenLit

TeenLit publishes poetry, essays, short stories, and book reviews from teen writers. They're open to adding new genres and ideas, too. The Web site features a discussion forum and writer's workshop.

www.speakuppress.org

Speak Up

Speak Up is a national nonprofit print literary journal that provides a creative voice for young adults (ages thirteen to nineteen years) through publication of their original fiction, nonfiction, poetry, plays, photography, and artwork. Annual.

www.mystworld.com/youngwriter/index.html

Young Writer

Young Writer is an international print magazine, run from Britain, featuring the best in English language creative writing (fiction, nonfiction, and poetry) from children aged five to eighteen from around the world. Although it accepts work from people up to age eighteen, the Web content seems to be mostly from children and young teenagers.

www.zuzu.org

ZuZu

ZuZu was a bimonthly newspaper for New York City kids and teens from 1992 until 1995. Since the print version folded, it has stayed alive on the Internet. ZuZu is filled with the images and words of kids of all ages from many different backgrounds.

It also features children's book writers and illustrators, profiles of adults engaged in a variety of interesting careers, and more stories that reflected young readers' interests. Bimonthly.

www.aboutteens.org
About Teens
About Teens features humorous photos and jokes, as well as short fiction, real life experiences, poetry, and book reviews—all written for and by teenagers. Monthly.

www.guidepostssweet16mag.com
Guideposts for Teens
This is the online counterpart to *Guideposts for Teens,* a magazine for Christian teens. In addition to teens' true-life stories, there are quizzes, advice columns on various topics, and articles on teen issues like dating, religion, volunteering, music, and school.

www.cosmogirl.com
CosmoGIRL!
This is the web site for *CosmoGirl*'s print magazine, aimed at teen girls. On the site's FAQ section there's information about applying to be a CosmoGirl teen contributor, as well as advice on getting internships at this magazine and others. Monthly.

www.cricketmag.com/ProductDetail.asp?pid=11
Cicada
Cicada, a market that sometimes pays for submissions, is a literary magazine for teenagers (aged fourteen and up). This is

the Web site, complete with submission guidelines, for the print magazine. *Cicada* publishes fiction short stories, poetry, and first-person essays by and for teens.

www.newmoon.org
New Moon Magazine for Girls
New Moon, which bills itself as the "smart feminist girl's magazine" publishes fiction, poetry, artwork, and letters by girls ages eight to fourteen. This is the Web site (including writer's guidelines) for the print magazine.

www.kidsonlinemagazine.com
Kids Online Magazine
This online magazine is like a traditional magazine with articles, stories, recipes, crafts, and artwork, but it exists on the Internet, it is written entirely by kids, and it is absolutely free. Monthly.

www.frodosnotebook.com
Frodo's Notebook
In addition to showcasing young writers before a large international audience, this site connects teens interested in literature and art with input and wisdom from adults already in the established literary scene, including professional writers, publishers, college professors, and its own editors.

http://members.aol.com/potluckmagazine/
Potluck Children's Literary Magazine
Potluck Magazine is a print magazine that publishes poetry,

short stories, fables, book reviews, and artwork by young writers ages eight to sixteen. Every submission, whether accepted for publication or not, receives a personal response and critique.

www.tywc.tk
The Young Writer's Community: Think, Read, Write
This site was founded and is still managed by a group of young writers. It features resources, tips, articles, and a forum for posting work.

www.teenwritersdream.com
A Teen Writer's Dream
This site features regular contests (winners get published in their poetry anthologies), as well as a forum for young writers to share their work and to get recognized for being published elsewhere.

www.bluejeanonline.com
Blue Jean Online
Blue Jean Online is a Web site written and produced by young women from around the world. It's a creative space for young women ages fourteen to twenty-two to submit their writings, reviews, artwork, photography, crafts, and other works for online publication to a worldwide audience.

www.fazeteen.com
Faze Magazine
This Web site is the online version of *Faze,* a magazine pub-

lished for young Canadians. Faze offers its readers insightful looks at real life issues, youth culture, and personal style, as well as the opportunity to submit their own creative fiction and poetry.

http://Web2.airmail.net/def/
Kidscribe
Kidscribe is a bilingual (English-Spanish) site dedicated to showcasing kids' writing and giving young authors confidence, personal pride, and cross-cultural respect.

www.stonesoup.com
Stone Soup
Stone Soup is unique among children's magazines—not only because it pays its writers, but because it's the only magazine made up entirely of the creative work of children. Young people from all over the world contribute their stories, poems, book reviews, and artwork to *Stone Soup*. At first, it's hard to believe eight- to thirteen-year-olds can create such engrossing stories, evocative poems, and gorgeous illustrations. But as regular readers of *Stone Soup* know—they can!

www.highlights.com
Highlights
For more than fifty years, *Highlights for Children* has left an indelible imprint on the hearts and minds of tens of millions of children. It has improved reading skills; it has helped define and develop values like honesty, thoughtfulness and tolerance; and it has entertained and enlightened. This Web site contains

a history of the magazine and detailed contributor guidelines. Important point: this market pays writers who are fifteen or older.

http://groups.yahoo.com/group/teenwritercoffeeshop/
Teen Writer Coffee Shop
This is the place for any teen who likes to write. You can post your work, get help when you've got writers' block, or just hang out, relax and read others' work.

http://dmoz.org/Kids_and_Teens/School_Time/English/Writing/
Open Directory of Teen Writing Resources

ADULTS HELPING TEEN WRITERS

Adults can help writers in various ways. These Web sites are places for writers of all ages, and most have their own spot especially made for teens.

www.writersdigest.com
Writer's Digest
You might have read the magazine, but have you ever been to the Web site? Visit it to see what's being featured in the magazine right now, enter contests and view the market of the day.

www.authorlink.com/605003in.html

Advice to Aspiring Young Writers

Although it is only a Web page, this article provides valuable advice on one page. It is worth reading and book marking for future reference since it is basic advice that all writers need.

www.pele.cx/~nonny/evolution

Evolution Writer's Community

This Web site has essays related to writing and being a writer. The main area of activity is on its discussion forums, which are set up so that both teen writers and adult writers are equal.

www.hollylisle.com

HollyLisle.com

Holly Lisle is a full-time writer sharing her experiences with other writers. On her site, you'll be able to find dozens of writing articles, a free e-book on writing, and advice that writers of all ages can use.

www.fmwriters.com

Forward Motion Writer's Community

This is a writer's community branching out from Holly Lisle.com. Besides the valuable information, classes, and challenges, you'll find an area made especially for young writers.

www.writersspot.com

WriteSpot

WriteSpot International has one main goal—to publish as many new authors as possible. Want to be one of them? To read the guidelines, check out their Web site.

www.writersmarkets.com

Writers Weekly

This Web site is a community and network for all writers. It has tips, markets, forums, interview requests—all the inside info.

www.eliteskills.com

Elite Skills Writing

Elite Skills is a nonprofit writers' community where users can sign up free and improve their writing skills through feedback and reading the works of others. There's a lot of poetry, but some fiction prose and lyrics as well.

www.writingcorner.com

Writing Corner

Writing Corner is an online resource for writers, readers and authors. From the ads on the site, it seems mostly focused on the romance genre, but it offers lots of advice and help (including links) for all kinds of writers.

www.write.org

WritingClasses.com

Teaching more than six thousand students a year, Gotham Writers' Workshop is the largest and most comprehensive creative writing school in New York City and online. It offers classes for young writers, too.

www.elizabethwinthrop.com/advice.html
Elizabeth Winthrop's Advice for Young Writers
This Web site offers advice from Elizabeth Winthrop, author of *The Castle in the Attic* and *The Battle in the Castle,* for young people on writing and getting published. Her site also has a message board for kids, parents, and teachers.

www.rejectioncollection.com
The Rejection Collection
The Rejection Collection is a site where writers can share their "sob stories" of rejection (and maybe even win a prize for Reject of the Month). It also features a newsletter and inspirational stories—even famous people fail sometimes!

http://cat.middlebury.edu/~neywc/
New England Young Writers' Conference
This is the Web site for a weekend conference for young writers at Middlebury College's Breadloaf campus in Vermont.

www.uiowa.edu/~iyws/
The Iowa Young Writers' Studio
Every summer, young writers from across the country come together to share their work, practice craft, and improve their writing in a program at the University of Iowa. Find out just how much you can improve your own writing with two weeks of intensive focus.

www.montesolworkshop.org

Monte Sol Workshop

The Monte Sol Workshop is a two-week summer residential program for high-school students who are passionate about becoming better writers and more insightful thinkers. Monte Sol provides a congenial community where students can expand their creative and analytical talents with peers who share their love for language.

Index

About the Authors

ELIZABETH HARPER is 2004 graduate of Ridgewood (N.J.) High School, where she was an honor student, all-county musician, National Merit Scholar, and an editor of *High Times*, the award-winning school newspaper. Author of the "High School Beat" column for the weekly *Ridgewood News*, her writing credits include *The New York Times* and op-ed pieces in *The Record*, the leading daily newspaper in northern New Jersey. Her copy-editing and proofreading credits include the upcoming personal-finance book, *Randy Neumann's Fighting for Your Financial Life*, and a series of Western novels by L. L. Layman. She has also worked as an assistant for best-selling mystery/suspense author Harlan Coben. She attends Oberlin College in Oberlin, Ohio.

TIMOTHY HARPER is a journalist, author, and editorial/publishing consultant based at *www.timharper.com*. A former national correspondent for the Associated Press, his eleven previous books include *Moscow Madness, License to Steal, Doing Good,* and *The ASJA Guide to Freelance Writing.* He has contributed hundreds of articles to magazines and newspapers around the world, including *The Atlantic Monthly, Reader's Digest, Sky,* the *International Herald Tribune, The New York Times, Chicago Tribune,* and many others. A member of the adjunct faculty at the Columbia University Graduate School of Journalism, he has served as a writing coach and corporate communications consultant for Time Inc., Newsweek, Intel, Pfizer, Alcoa, and various Wall Street firms. As a publishing consultant and collaborator, he helps individuals and corporations write books and get them published. He is also a partner in BooksByBookends (www.booksbybookends.com), the first in-bookstore self-publishing print-on-demand service in America.